T0196135

THE BUSINESS PLAN
FOR HAPPINESS

ANTHONY PETERS

authorHOUSE®

AuthorHouse™ UK Ltd.
500 Avebury Boulevard
Central Milton Keynes, MK9 2BE
www.authorhouse.co.uk
Phone: 08001974150

Published by AuthorHouse 4/23/2013

ISBN: 978-1-4772-4610-8 (sc)
ISBN: 978-1-4772-4611-5 (e)

ACKNOWLEDGEMENTS

Thanks to my parents for their unconditional love and support. I am blessed to have you both.

Thanks to Geshe Kelsang Gyatso and all those at *Discovering the Heart of Buddhism* for continuing to turn the Wheel Of Dharma: *www.buddhism-connect.org*

Thanks to Barefoot Doctor, Stephen Russell who has been an inspiration: *www.barefootdoctorglobal.com*

Very special thanks and much love to Trevina, Pauly and Emma R. Your help has been invaluable.

TABLE OF CONTENTS

Introduction ix

Preface

    The Business Plan For Happiness: Overview 1

    Executive Summary 3

    Business Description 5

    Rationale 7

    Financial Forcast 9

    How This Business Plan For Happiness Works 11

Home: Happiness Begins At Home 15

Home: Be On The Cause Side Of Life 25

Home: Positivity Creates High Happiness Income 35

Home: Negative Media 45

Home: You Create Your Own Reality 51

Home: Understanding Others 63

Rest: The Importance Of Meditation 67

Work: What Role Does Money Play? 77

Work: Creating Happiness At Work 81

Work: The Importance Of Meaning And Purpose 85

Work: Strengthen Your Strengths 91

Work: The Lab Profile 95

Work: Spreading Happiness 107

Play: Pay Attention 111

    •   Creating a State Of Flow 115

    •   Savouring 119

Play: Be Social 123

Play: Move Your Bad Self 125

    •   Exercise Exertion Scale 134

End Note 135

About the Author 139

References 141

INTRODUCTION

"Happiness is the meaning and the purpose of life, the whole aim and end of human existence."

Aristotle

THIS BOOK IS FOR anyone wanting to know how to increase their life satisfaction, well-being and happiness.

This is a book for every single person on the planet because gaining more happiness is the ultimate gift.

All you really want from life is to be happy. At the end of your days, if you can say that you have been truly happy, then your life will have been fulfilled and worthwhile regardless of whether you find yourself in a large house with opulent furnishings or a modest home with very little. In this sense, attaining lasting happiness is the ultimate goal in life.

What makes you happy? What makes you *lastingly* happy? Can you learn to be happier?

Shortly after returning from holiday in 2002, I booked myself in for an annual health check at the doctors. It was an early appointment and I was sleepy when I met with the doctor, which I blame for the random question I asked. Whilst having the usual blood pressure and cholesterol tests, I asked my doctor if he knew how I could be happier. I don't quite know what I expected as a reply because I knew it was a strange question when I said it. The doctor stuttered whilst he considered the question before asking if I was depressed.

I explained that I wasn't depressed and that I felt contented with my stable job, the roof over my head and I had food on the table, good friends and loving family but I still wondered if there was something I could do to boost happiness. The doctor discussed herbal and pharmaceutical pills that could help, but for me that was cheating. There must be a real way to become happier I thought.

Not quite knowing how to answer my awkward question and suspecting I was depressed, the doctor referred me a psychologist. Out of curiosity I took up the referral.

A couple of weeks later I met with the psychologist and her opening statements were to ask me about my "depression". I corrected her and explained that I was not depressed, in fact, I was relatively happy but I wanted to know how to amplify my happiness. I asked if she knew of any research into the 'how' of happiness but she didn't. She knew how to reduce and help eliminate depression, anxiety and posttraumatic disorders but not how to make a person happier.

What is happiness? It's not merely the absence of depression or anxiety. What makes someone happy? Why are some people happier than others? Are there techniques that can increase levels of happiness? Are there different types of happiness?

Finding the answers to these questions has been my quest for the past decade. I have studied countless research papers and numerous academic books from some of the leading scientist in the field of behaviour change, applied Positive Psychology and Neuro-linguistic Programming (NLP). I have literally made happiness my business.

From my research I have found that you *can* increase your happiness. There *are* practical tools and techniques that will significantly improve your sense of well-being, give you more resilience when times are tough, improve your self-esteem and provide you with a greater degree of life satisfaction. This book will show you how.

I work with hundreds of individuals each year to help increase their well-being and resolve barriers to happiness through the incorporation of techniques that really work (www.wisemonkeytraining.co.uk).

The Business Plan For happiness will introduce you to the evidence and provide you with the key foundational tools that will increase your lasting happiness.

THE BUSINESS PLAN FOR HAPPINESS: OVERVIEW

*"Life has no meaning. Each of us has meaning and we bring it to life.
It is a waste to be asking the question when you are the answer."*
Joseph Campbell

A SUCCESSFUL BUSINESS PLAN should be well thought out and this one is supported by the very latest scientific evidence in the field of Positive Psychology.

A solid business plan should be clear and concise so the aim of this book is to identify areas of maximum happiness profit with minimal expenditure in effort and time.

A successful business plan should have a logical structure that is easy to follow and be efficacious. This Business Plan for Happiness is laid out in four universally identifiable and interrelated target areas of: HOME, REST, WORK and PLAY

This business plan must show you how to make your business of happiness successful. It will therefore identify and highlight what the evidence shows you can do to maximise your income of lasting happiness.

To be a success in your life, your business of happiness must make profit and this book will lay out precise evidence based practical techniques that will make you happier.

Providing you follow the business plan using the structured, clear and concise methods indicated, and stick to the practical methods, you will gain increased lasting happiness. This will be your true profit in life

EXECUTIVE SUMMARY

*"The most important thing is to enjoy your life —
to be happy — it's all that matters."*
Audrey Hepburn

THIS BOOK IS STRUCTURED as a business plan to help you create much more happiness in life. Not the fleeting happiness that comes from doing the things you enjoy - although this has its place - but focus will be given to significantly increasing your *lasting* day-to-day level of happiness.

Founded on groundbreaking research in the scientific field of Positive Psychology, this book lays out what you can do to increase your lasting happiness at home, at rest, at work and at play.

Everyone wants to be happy all day, every day. Happiness is the true currency of your life and having more money or more material possession will not increase levels of happiness but may actually reduce it. Hard though it may be to comprehend, if you won millions on the lottery your best method for achieving lasting happiness is to give the majority of it away.

If money and material possessions do not provide you with incrementally more happiness, what is the true currency of life?

Any business plan will target identified market areas to maximise revenue and financial profit. Therefore, this book lays out ways to create, invest and generate the real, true currency in life: happiness.

BUSINESS DESCRIPTION

"Human resources are like natural resources; they're often buried deep. You have to go looking for them, they're not just lying around on the surface. You have to create the circumstances where they show themselves."
Ken Robinson

THE STRUCTURED AND DETAILED practical techniques within this book will cost you in terms of time and effort, but this investment will be exceeded by the return in happiness. Using this approach to increase your happiness in a structured and targeted manner will create happiness profit.

You will learn how to reduce bad investments (negative affect) and significantly increase good investments (positive affect) so you invest wisely and become wealthy in well-being and happiness.

All good business plans start with a solid rationale to answer the following:

- Why you think your business will work?
- What market is there which gives you reason to think you can make a good and meaningful life out of your investments (effort and time)?
- What are your target areas to bring in the most income?
- What evidence do you have to believe your business model is worthwhile?

As this *is* a good business plan providing you with the most rewarding and valuable currency of all – increased lasting happiness – we will start with the rationale.

RATIONALE

*"We all live with the objective of being happy; our
lives are all different and yet the same."*

Anne Frank

ESSENTIALLY THERE ARE TWO types of happiness: 1) Momentary
(Hedonic) happiness; and 2) Lasting (Eudiamonic) happiness.[75, 109, 119]
Momentary happiness is the short lived happiness that can vary
in degrees of intensity and typically triggered by a situation or context
such the a feeling of happiness experienced whilst relaxing in the bath,
having sex or basking in the sunshine. Nice though it is to experience,
they differ from lasting happiness because thcy are momentary.
Alternatively, lasting happiness is the underlying, consistent level of
overall contentment and well-being you can experience on any given
day at any given time, like a foundation of happiness within you.

What makes you momentarily happy is subjective and personal to
you. If it is healthy and has positive benefits to you and harms no one,
then you will know how to increase this already by simply doing more
of it. However, this is not lasting happiness. Having a few glasses of
wine in the evening may bring you a sense of momentary happiness but
soon that feeling will fade towards sobriety and a hangover. Watching a
movie may bring you momentary happiness but invest more and more
time in this pursuit and you will become bored and listless. Eating a
piece of cake may bring you momentary happiness but eat it all and you
will soon feel sick. Increased investment, in terms of time and effort,
in these types of hedonic pleasures will not bring you the equivalent
income of happiness.

Time spent in your hedonic pleasures is great as long as it is virtuous
and does not harm you or anyone else, but this Business Plan for

Happiness is not aimed at building your hedonic, momentary happiness. Used as a foundation in your happiness business plan, seeking more hedonic happiness is flawed and doomed for bankruptcy.

This business plan must be focused on what you can do to continually add to your lasting happiness with minimal increase in expenditure of effort and time.

Your business projection is to grow your lasting happiness throughout your life so that it becomes prosperous and flourishing.

With a solid foundation of lasting happiness in your life, your business of happiness will not only give brighter colour to your day when times are good, it will also help increase your ability to cope and find resilience when times are tough.[17, 57, 95] By raising your level of lasting happiness you are very likely to live a longer,[27, 39] healthier,[106] flourishing,[58] successful[88] and satisfied life.[69,108]

Research suggests that fifty percent of your lasting happiness is innate and based on a genetic predisposition and there is little you can do about that. Ten percent is circumstantial and based on the type of environment you live in, which to some degree, is in your control but typically hard to change. However, a whopping forty percent of your lasting happiness is completely down to your mindset and within your own control[107]. With a little effort and practical application, this control is relatively easy to achieve and can be set permanently for the rest of your life.[109]

Most people see money as a means to increased happiness but the rationale of this business plan holds that money provides momentary happiness, which does not last.

Do not give up on making money because it has its place within your Business Plan for Happiness but understand from the start that the real investment towards happiness will come from other sources.

The true and lasting happiness you seek in your life can only come from the thoughts, actions and behaviours you invest into your daily activities within your home, at rest, whilst at play and during your working day.

Money does little to increase your lasting happiness and so this business plan is based around researched practical tools you can use to gain the thing you wish for, want and strive for in your life: maximum lasting happiness.

FINANCIAL FORCAST

"I can't change the direction of the wind, but I can adjust my sails to always reach my destination."
Jimmy Dean

YOU MUST BE DEDICATED to make your Business Plan for Happiness work and believe in your product. You must stick to the business plan and put in the effort and time, especially within the initial months, in order for it to be a success. In the initial stages you must be absolutely determined to stick to the plan, practise the techniques in a structured and diligent manner in order to grow and nurture your lasting happiness.

Most new businesses will fail within the first year so make a decision now to have continuous and unwavering belief in yourself and the product of lasting happiness.

With this mindset your happiness business will ultimately develop to the point where things happen by themselves; 'orders' will come in from all the 'contacts' you have made through the regular practise of techniques. You will have made adjustments and adaptations to find out areas of happiness that work best for you and suit your lifestyle. Effort will decrease as working practice becomes a normal daily routine and a natural way of doing 'business'. Eventually, you will be the Managing Director of your own happiness business and it will flow in abundance as the business thrives with minimal effort.

By the time you have finished reading this Business Plan for Happiness you will know how to make well-being and lasting happiness easy.

Once you have read the entire book you must take action. Immediately choose one technique and practise it with a constant focus on the overall goal to achieve maximum profit of happiness. Once you are confident that this practise has become a part of your routine, you can move onto the next technique.

Businesses fail by poor management of income against expenses and therefore, it is essential for you to get this balance right. Enthusiasm is to be commended but be aware of expending too much too soon. Invest your time and effort in what you can 'afford' right now and reap the rewards of that investment until the income is consistent and easily maintained before moving onto another target area of happiness investment.

Bearing in mind that it takes around one month to create a new habit[85] this is not a quick fix business plan. To make your income of happiness lasting and your business of happiness a lifelong success, you must be prepared to spend around twelve to sixteen months gradually layering each target area methodically until it becomes an automatic way of doing things.

It is important to note that it will not take this length of time to feel and see the happiness return, it will occur much sooner. Many of the techniques will bring an almost instant income of happiness. To make happiness your successful business at home, at rest, at work and at play, you must invest wisely; timely implementing each strategy until it becomes woven into your very being and becomes effortless.

It should be noted that there will be lots of interlinking areas or 'cross-selling' of techniques. For example, practising techniques to increase positivity can be used in all four target areas. These techniques have been divided merely to help focus and organise your business of happiness into definable areas. All areas are interlinked and practising all techniques will create an overflow of happiness across all aspects of your life.

HOW THIS BUSINESS PLAN
FOR HAPPINESS WORKS

"I keep remembering one of my Guru's teachings about happiness. She says that people universally tend to think that happiness is a stroke of luck, something that will maybe descend upon you like fine weather if you're fortunate enough. But that's not how happiness works. Happiness is the consequence of personal effort. You fight for it, strive for it and insist upon it. You have to participate relentlessly in the manifestations of your own blessings. And once you have achieved a state of happiness, you must never become lax about maintaining it, you must make a mighty effort to keep swimming upward into that happiness forever, to stay afloat on top of it."

Elizabeth Gilbert.
Eat, Pray, Love

LIKE ANY GOOD BUSINESS plan, you must start by looking at what capital (resources, time and effort) you initially have available to you as you set up your business. What areas can you afford to start working on now to get the happiness 'cash' coming in?

At the end this book, you can find a technique summary table. To help organise and choose a logical and methodical method of working through the techniques, each is rated in terms of judged Initial Effort Rating (I.E.R) verses Happiness Income Rating (H.I.R).

On the technique summary table you will see two columns by each technique, one named "I.E.R" and the other named "H.I.R".

The I.E.R column is left blank for you to rate how much each technique will cost you in terms of the initial effort you believe the technique will require from you. The I.E.R is based on your own judgement of time commitment needed to implement the technique, the level of difficulty based on your current lifestyle and circumstances and the effort you believe it will take. After you have read each chapter, complete your estimation of I.E.R for all techniques within that chapter. Once you have finished the book you will have a list of all techniques that can be ranked in order of lowest I.E.R. (subjective rating of least initial effort needed) through to highest I.E.R (subjective rating of most initial effort needed). Having an organised ranking of techniques you will be able to start with your 'easiest' techniques and, over the months, you can work your way through to those that take a little more effort. Rate your I.E.R from 1 to 10. 1 meaning no effort at all. 10 meaning lots of effort.

The reason for this is two-fold: 1) You are far more likely to continue and remain motivated with your Business Plan for Happiness if you start with the techniques you feel would be most enjoyable and easiest to implement; 2) As you introduce those techniques with the lowest I.E.R at the start, your income of happiness will accumulate and increase your resources to continue with the remaining techniques.

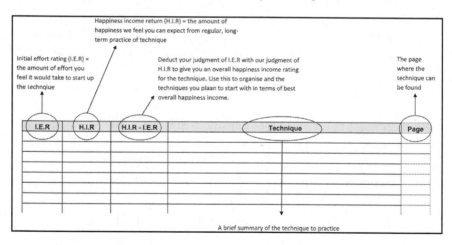

The second column indicates the amount of points, rated 1 to 10 of H.I.R. H.I.R. represents the expected return in amount of happiness you can gain from mastering the described technique. H.I.R is an arbitrary guide but based on the evidence to help you quantify and prioritise the happiness income you will earn from practising the technique.

Looking through your rated techniques, I suggest you begin with the techniques providing lower I.E.R and higher H.I.R so that you can start your new business of happiness with ease (low I.E.R) and yet also experience happiness cash flow quickly (high H.I.R).

For example, research shows that meditation provides many avenues of happiness income through decreased stress, improved health, increased ability to cope, improved sense of well-being and connection with others. Meditation has therefore been given a H.I.R of 10. However, your current life situation may be such that you judge the I.E.R for meditation as 8 at this moment in time so that your overall happiness income (= H.I.R – I.E.R) would be only 2. In this example, the overall happiness rating may move meditation down on your priority list. Perhaps you have just moved house and you have all the unpacking and settling in to do. You have the kids to sort out and make sure they get settled in their new school and home. Perhaps, even though you recognise that fifteen minutes meditation every day would bring in lots of happiness income and help you cope with the changes, you may also recognise that you would rather focus on another target area of happiness income until your life is more stable.

When you finish this book you will have rated all techniques, listed them in order of overall happiness income (H.I.R – I.E.R) so you can identify techniques that you can introduce with ease and that will also bring in happiness for yourself. Essentially this is the same as assessing your business model and looking at what target areas will bring in most capital with minimal expenditure.

Spreading your investment across all target areas fully is going to bring your life the most happiness so incorporating all techniques over time is highly recommended.

Spend around four weeks implementing each individual technique into your life before choosing the next one. Do not forget to keep the other techniques going because they will be crucial in maintaining a lasting income of happiness and will keep your happiness - and even financial - bank topped up.

With initial effort your income of happiness will be flowing and you will soon enjoy an abundance of well-being profit.

HOME: HAPPINESS BEGINS AT HOME

*"The basic root of happiness lies in our minds; outer circumstances
are nothing more than adverse or favourable."*
Matthieu Ricard

THE TERM "HOME" IN this section refers to the traditional concept of home life and how to increase the currency of happiness at home and in your family. However, the adage of: "Happiness begins at home" is also taken as meaning within yourself. If you are not happy within your own skin, unhappy with who you are or believing that you do not deserve to be happy, then all other investments will provide minimal return. Happiness is something that is created within you and therefore, if you do not believe or have faith in the product your entire business is founded on, how can you expect to build on it or invest your time and effort into it?

Research suggests that climate, environmental and even financial circumstances do little to increase lasting happiness.[72] Therefore, it is helpful to understand the benefits of the 'lasting happiness coin'.

Imagine you are given a lasting happiness coin. This is a magic coin that you can put in your pocket and carry with you wherever you go. As long as you have this coin you will experience more happiness than those without it. The lasting happiness coin creates inner well-being, inner contentment, love and enjoyment. Without the lasting happiness coin it will not matter where you go, whether you are in a hot climate or lush green pastures, if you are not carrying the coin your happiness level will remain unchanged. You have the potential to possess the happiness coin and there are things you can do to be sure you carry it everywhere.

The HOME chapter will mostly refer to the happiness gained by adjusting your behaviour. Unless you can make your internal 'home' happy, finding lasting happiness will be very hard. It will be like throwing good happiness investments into a poorly advised and poorly managed bank.

Would you buy a car from a dealer who badmouths and points out all the faults in the cars he shows you? Similarly, how can you expect to make happiness your income if you do not believe you can make this business of happiness work?

The key to lasting happiness is not found in things *outside* of you. The key to lasting happiness starts with things *inside* of you.

To start with you must rediscover yourself and find who you really are. You must accept yourself, build and broaden our strengths whilst letting go of your weaknesses.

> *"We need to reconnect with our true self in our lives."*
> **Vitterso**

You are born like a perfect jewel, pristine and immaculate. The perfect jewel has no negative views of you. A baby and a young child have limited self-concept and can therefore live in the moment and be free to be true to themselves without fear of judgement from others. The child engages in activities that make them happy in that moment. As an adult you lose that connection, you become too conscious of what others may think and conform to who you think you should be rather than being your perfect self and the jewel you were born as.

> *"The realisation of human potential is an ultimate goal."*
> **Aristotle**

We will begin by helping to find and reconnect with your jewel-like-self and your true nature.

As you grow in early childhood, your experiences begin to form a concept of self. Strong feelings of negativity are created from the spiteful speech, thoughtless minds, jealous tongues and the big egos of other people.

Experiences that create the largest level of negativity will stick with you and you may have found yourself re-living the moment by playing the situation over in your mind. These negative experiences create layers of beliefs, begin to set personal limitations and negative perception of yourself.

The more you think and behave in a certain way, the more likely you will form a link between your negative experiences and who you think you are as a person. You were not born with these beliefs but your mind will have created negative and limiting beliefs through a cycle of thought, feeling and behaviour. This cycle results in the creation of our self-perception.

We will refer to this created self-perception as your mind-created-self.

Think of a very young child and recognise how they have minimal conscious feelings of what other people think when they dance or play. Young children are free to live and laugh as they wish because they have not yet developed a concept of self. It is only through the creation of their mind-created-self that the child begins to become self-aware and consider how others might view them.

As time passes your jewel-self begins to unwittingly gather more experiences, some will be positive and others will be negative. These experiences feed into your developing mind-created-self until you began to believe that you *are* those feelings and that your negative experiences are caused by your own imperfections rather than the reality which is the other way round.

This happens with us all and we gradually lose sight of the free spirited, carefree child we were born as. As we grow, feelings of self-consciousness then reinforce the existence of our mind-created-self and our jewel-self gradually disappears.

Over time, we gather more negative experiences, which begin to weigh us down - metaphorically speaking - until we begin to feel unhappy. We begin to accept that we are 'faulty' in small ways or not comfortable in certain situations. Our perfect, carefree jewel becomes smothered in dirt (negative baggage).

In evolutionary terms your negative emotions would have been of more use. Negative emotions created from the experiences of our ancestors, such as fear, would have served to protected them from danger. Anger would have given them the aggression to fight off threats, protect bloodline and pass on strong genes. Negative emotions drove our prehistoric family away from negative situations and aided their survival. Through avoidance, aversion and aggression, our ancestral negative emotions would have been helpful to our survival.

In the modern day, with rarely anything to fight or run from, negative emotions have a tendency to be turned inwards on ourselves and we associate the negative experiences as something to avoid, express aggression towards or run away from.

What do your negative emotions drive you away from? Achieving your potential in life perhaps?

On the one hand you want to feel different and achieve all your wishes and fulfil your goal in life but on the other hand you cannot control the negative feelings that drive you away or hold you back. This incongruence between your internal mind-created-self and your want to express your true jewel-like-self, can make you feel torn, frustrated or unhappy; saying: *"I wish I could..."*

Lasting happiness is defined as being fulfilled and realising your true potential. This occurs when your life activities are most in line with your deep values.[119] On the one hand, your jewel-self will know what you can achieve in life but on the other hand, you have negative emotions that layer dirt on your jewel-like-self. It is easier to believe your negative mind-created-self rather than to do what your jewel-like-self knows you can achieve. This conflict is what holds you back from attaining your true potential. It follows that you consciously and unconsciously attempt to change yourself in order to resolve this internal conflict.

In an attempt to change yourself 'for the better', you may disguise your dirt covered jewel in varnish so that you appear to feel better. You may attempt to cover up your 'weaknesses' so that others do not notice your perceived dirt/ faults. The varnish typically used comes in the form of misplaced pride, acting falsely, trying to be like someone else and using clothes or vanity to cover your mind-created perception of self.

Think of your own experiences and remember a time when you dismissed or ignored certain negative comments from other people without any impact on you. Although unaffected by some comments, you are equally as likely to remember feeling deeply offended, angry or self-conscious about other negative comments. Why is this?

It is due to the varnish you have put on yourself or, more accurately, the perceived lack of varnish that has allowed someone to see through it and to your 'imperfections'.

For example, you may feel completely at ease with the way you look and so jokes and fun made by others towards your looks provoke little reaction or fail to upset you. However, if you are self-conscious about the way you look your mind-created-self becomes strong when teased by others and instead of laughing with them you feel and react very differently.

Your mind-created-self has a need to hide the perceived dirt it carries causing you to act defensively, aggressively or feel negatively towards yourself when the reality is you are a truly amazing and beautiful jewel who holds untold potential. Silly comments or negative actions from other people should mean nothing to you because you are perfect just as you are.

IDENTIFYING YOUR BAGGAGE

As a general rule, when you feel defensive or aggravated by someone or when anger takes hold from a comment from someone else, you should stop and assess your emotions. Ask yourself if your emotion are justified, or is it due to the baggage you carry? If you are honest with yourself and you find the latter is true, this is a good lesson learnt and you can recognise your baggage and your mind-created-self and work to let it go and wash off the varnish.

As you reconnect with your true self your self-esteem can increase. Having an appropriate level of self-esteem is beneficial because low self-esteem is associated with depression, psychological compulsions, obsessions and poor health behaviours such as smoking and excessive alcohol consumption.[76] Individuals with high levels of self-esteem tend to have greater psychological resilience and show more perseverance even in situations where they are unlikely to succeed.[69]

Individuals rated with high levels of self-esteem also report higher levels of intelligence and happiness although some individuals who report high levels of self-esteem show less resilience and are prone to anger and aggression. These latter people are likely to be using their inflated concept of self-esteem as varnish and will appear to be confident and secure but in reality are highly sensitive. As a means to protect them when challenged or when their varnished cover is blown, they become angry, defensive and will tend to divert blame.[69]

You may also try and cover up your 'imperfections' in an attempt to change them or in an effort to make them disappear but covering up a stain on the carpet with a rug or turning your back on it does not mean the stain disappears, however, it has the potential to cause you to feel even more self-conscious when someone sees or mentions it. If you attempt to use more 'varnish' to cover your negative baggage in the hope that they will change you, someone will spot it in the end.

WATCH YOUR BAD SELF

Never judge the seemingly inappropriate actions and behaviours of others. Do not forget that by judging someone you are doing exactly what has fed and formed your own mind-created-self. Check your own negative reactions and identify those that are associated with your own use of varnish and simply let go. Be yourself with nothing to hide. If you do not do this, your negative thoughts and feelings about yourself and others will play out to become reality.

Imagine falling over dramatically in full view of strangers. The situation typically causes feelings of slight embarrassment or stronger feelings of shame. The only reason such feelings arise is because the mind-created-self will have you believe that other people are thinking negative thoughts about you and it may even create negative thoughts about yourself too; saying: *"You look like a fool. Everyone will be thinking you're an idiot. You are an idiot"* The negative comments made in your mind and the assumption of other people's perception of you is purely mind created and not fact. In reality, people may laugh not because they think the person who tripped and fell is innately silly or foolish but because their own mind-created-self is relieved it was not them.

When something potentially embarrassing happens to someone I stop myself from laughing - unless they quite clearly find it funny themselves - and I always say something like: *"I did that same thing yesterday"* or *"I've seen so many people do exactly the same thing"*. By saying this, I am trying to help the person realise that their 'embarrassing' action is not a flaw in their make-up or personality. This also helps them forget or dismiss any negative thoughts their mind-created-self may be saying and prevents them creating or adding negative baggage to their jewel-like-self.

Have continuous compassion for others because, ultimately, we all want to be happy.

The ability to adaptively perceive, understand, regulate and harness emotions in yourself and others is known as emotional intelligence[65] and is very helpful on the road to lasting happiness. Having a good level of emotional intelligence will enable you to cope with social situations and deal compassionately with other people whilst remaining kind hearted and in control of your own mind-created-self.

You were not born with negative baggage; the dirt is there because of your mind-created-self, and you are not your mind-created-self. Your mind-created-self is nothing more than a collection of thoughts and experiences that you can now let go of if you choose.

Realise that any negative feelings and thoughts are not who you really are but simply your mind-created-self. You can now let go of this unnecessary 'baggage'. Put down your negative baggage and walk away from it so now you feel lighter, more energised, gain more self-esteem and start to feel happy with who you really are: a perfect jewel with unlimited potential

---

FIVE STEPS TO INCREASE EMOTIONAL INTELLIGENCE

According to Goleman,[65] there are five main areas which should be considered when attempting to increase ones emotional intelligence:

1. The ability to manage your emotions by reframing anxiety and move away from feelings of distress.

2. Practice of delaying gratification in order to savour the experience and know that reward will come with patience.

3. Recognise the emotions of others and understand them with appropriate empathy.

4. Through an empathetic understanding of other people's emotions, you can support them and empathise with them.

5. Last but by no means least, you must be aware of your own emotions, recognise that: a) you can never truly know the reasons why someone may say or do negative things towards you or others; and b) you were born as a perfect jewel and you still are, so don't listen to your mind-created-self, it's only function is to make you believe that you are faulty in some way and thus, it talks utter rubbish.

When you make mistakes, misunderstand things, misinterpret things, make foolish comments or simply trip and fall in public, see it as human behaviour and nothing more. Laugh at your behaviour or smile and dismiss any negative thoughts immediately. Who cares?!

The only thing who cares what other people might think of you is your mind-created-self and it bases the assumptions on pure guesswork.

Your mind-created-self is your nemesis. Your mind-created-self has one role and that is to make you feel bad and make you forget all the things that make you special and unique.

"Life's an adventure, travel light"

You are much more in control of your-mind-self than you think and certainly more in control than the founder of psychoanalysis Sigmund Freud believed. Freud stated that all of our personality and behaviours could be explained and are driven by all past experiences. In fact, little evidence is found to support a major impact on adult life from childhood.[34, 54, 62] It would seem that children are much more resilient than we give them credit for and problems within childhood tend to significantly wane as you grow up. Surveys and longitudinal studies show that environment and traumas experienced within childhood do little to predict adult behaviour, personality or determine life direction. The main and overriding factor is shown to be genetics. Freud was incorrect and if you are blaming your childhood for your behaviour or your own life situation the truth that you are much more in control of your life than you think.

If you play to your perceived insecurities and the negative baggage you used to carry you are limiting yourself unnecessarily.

Accepting yourself and letting go of your perceived or real areas of 'weakness' is a major component towards positive psychological well-being (PWB)[103] and PWB is linked to happiness.[77]

Having a good level of self-acceptance aids a positive level of PWB, which improves overall level of well-being through probable causes such as increased focus on strengths rather than weaknesses. This will provide you with increased sense of purpose, personal growth and control.

It is only when you decide to 'wash off' all your 'dirt', surrender and let go of your ego and baggage, that you realise you are a perfect jewel and that it is only your mind that holds you back.

Next time you are feeling worried, angry, pressured, defensive or nervous, ask yourself why? What is the reason behind your feelings? Is it because of someone else's mind-created-self feeling threatened? Or is it because deep inside, your own mind-created-self is making you feel a need to protect itself due to the negative baggage it makes you carry?

Improve your emotional intelligence, recognise and cultivate your strengths and let go of your baggage.

HOME: BE ON THE CAUSE
SIDE OF LIFE

"Achieving genuine happiness may require bringing about a transformation in your outlook, your way of thinking, and this is not a simple matter."
His Holiness The 14th Dalai Lama

YOU HAVE FORTY PERCENT control over your happiness[86, 87,112] so be determined to promote well-being within your life. You will still have to do some of the things that you do not want to do but start to take note of how many of these things you can change or exchange for the behaviours you enjoy.

A conversation with my cousin about my work in positive psychology and his charity work in war torn and disaster stricken countries lead to a story about a man he met in Somalia. Somalia is a failed anarchic state, riddled with corruption, no structured government and famine is widespread. Somalia is one of the most dangerous places on earth and, according to my cousin, is one of the hardest, most miserable and deprived places to live.

My cousin recalled a man he met whilst working on the water supply to a small village outside of Mogadishu. This man had lost most of his family to either famine or murderous campaigns driven by drug gangs and civil war. He had learned to speak English from the World Service barely audible on his old crackling radio. He collected books from aid workers and practised his English with them. He had taught himself English to a level where my cousin could have in-depth conversations with him but he noted one strange habit; the man talked to a stone he kept in his pocket. It was his 'thank you stone' the man explained. It was a lucky stone given to him by his late father and it collected positive spirits. He would list the things he was grateful for every time he came across the stone in his pocket.

My cousin remembered this man because of his optimism and positivity. The Somali was optimistic that he would leave his village and one day live in England.

A few weeks after I was told this story, I found myself thinking about the Somali man and called my cousin to ask if he knew what happened to the man and his stone: *"Last time I heard he was living in England"* replied my cousin.

Those that believe they can't probably can't.
Those that believe they can probably can.

We hear of similar stories all the time, the most well-known is that of Sir Roger Bannister. Despite claims from fellow athletes and leading Physiologists that it was physically and anatomically *impossible* for the human body to run a sub-four minute mile, Sir Bannister believed he could. On May 6th in 1954 during the British Amateur athletics meet in Oxford, Sir Roger Bannister ran a mile in 3 minutes 59.4 seconds.

GATHER YOURSELF A GRATITUDE STONE

There are of course no magical powers found in a stone (or are there?) but the benefits of having a gratitude stone is profound.

Next time you are in the woods, forest or on the beach, find yourself a stone. Take your time to pick a good one that catches your eye or that you like. A stone small enough to carry around with you.

Keep this stone with you in your purse, wallet or in the pocket of the coat you wear frequently. Or place it somewhere that you will come across it frequently. I keep mine in my spare change jar (yes, I have a money pot jar and no, I'm not twelve years old!).

Everytime you come across it state five things that you are grateful for such as your health, the weather (rain gives us life, sunshine makes us feel nice), your job, your family, friends, loved ones or anything you are truly thankful to have.

Place your gratitude stone in a place where you will see or feel it regularly and verbally or mentally recite the things, people or feelings you can be grateful to have in your life.

If you believe that you are only here to get by and take the highs when they emerge amongst the abundance of lows before your life is over, then why not focus on the positives and make the most of everyday whilst you are still here because the research shows that if you think life is great, it will be.[10, 90]

Make the most of every day as if it were your last because if it does not make you happy, make a decision to make positive changes as soon as possible. This book will help you.

In a conversation you may believe that the words and gestures you are using are the correct ones to produce the desired response from the person you are talking to. E.g. explaining the meaning of life to help open their mind or directing them to the local shop to get some milk. However, if you do not get the response you expect from the conversation, you tend to blame the other person. You blame them believing that they did not understand what you were saying or that they were not listening properly. This assumption is based on the belief that a conversation between two people is a fifty/fifty split in responsibility. This view allows each individual to *give up* fifty percent of the responsibility to the other person, thus, when the desired outcome does not materialise from the conversation, and the person returns from the shop with a loaf of bread instead of milk, you will tend to blame them because they hold fifty percent of the responsibility.

There is a line in the film War Of The World's where Tom Cruise is playing the role of a father. Trying to convince the characters daughter that he can help her with her homework, he says: *"between me and my brother we know everything, so ask me anything you like."* So his daughter asks him what the capital of Australia is to which he replies: *"that's the one my brother knows!"*

This type of 'shared responsibility thinking' takes the control and responsibility away from what you get out of a conversation. If you think this way in other areas of your life then when you do not quite reach or attain your goals, desires and aspirations in life you believe that it is not due to your own behaviour, but due to the behaviour of others and events outside your control. You blame the other fifty percent. This type of thinking puts you on the 'effect' side of life and not the 'cause'. On the effect side of life you have no control and life is something that happens *to* you. Being on the cause side of life puts you in control and you become the master of how you live and how you shape your future.

When you move to the cause side and start to understand that each individual is <u>*one hundred percent*</u> responsible for the response and outcomes in their life, you realise that you are in control, you cause positive things in your life because you are responsible.

You could list events that you would say were completely out of your control but it is how you choose to view those events and respond to them which makes all the difference. You are one hundred percent in control of how you react and frame the outcome of an event, no matter how negative it is.

> *"Get busy living or get busy dying"*
> *(The Shawshank Redemption)*

Be an optimist because you will live longer.[39, 82,95] Being optimistic about a situation or your life, creates positive emotions, which supports healthy immune responses whilst also affecting the likelihood of you practising positive health behaviours such as giving up smoking and only drinking moderate levels of alcohol. Research shows that optimists are more likely to take action when needed to change their situation whereas pessimists will simply give up control.[106]

Having control makes you happier in life[102] and makes you achieve more.[53] If you feel out of control and unable to influence your situation, levels of happiness drop significantly. A sense of control over your life (along with self-esteem and optimism) is critical to your level of lasting happiness.[7, 93, 117] It is good to know that you are one hundred percent responsible for the responses you get out of your life and that you can work to be optimistic and see the 'silver lining' in any situation. If you do not get what you want, you are not 'communicating' correctly, so do not be a pessimist and give up, simply change your approach and move towards your goal once again. Not getting what you want is not due to other people but purely down to the way you are behaving and therefore a great opportunity to learn how to do things better.

As Billy Connolly says: *"There's no such thing as bad weather, just a bad choice of clothes"*

It is about how you respond to your environment, what you believe, how you behave and how you frame your thoughts that matter. Imagine yourself standing in shorts and T-shirt in the snow. In such a situation, it will only take a few moments before you start thinking that the weather is terrible, miserable and really chilly. However, put some gloves on, a winter coat, hat, thick socks, boots, thermals and scarf and you are off sledging, having fun in the snow. The change of clothes into more appropriate kit completely changes the way in which you view your experience. A change in the way you react and view things can likewise completely change the way you feel and behave in your life.

THREE STRATEGIES TO MAINTAIN CONTROL

Thompson (2002) proposes three key strategies to help you maintain control:

1. Make sure your goals are realistic and attainable within your current situation. If you've just had twins your goal to meditate for hours every day may need to be adjusted to 10 or 20 minutes a day for the time being.

2. If your current situation means that your goal is temporarily unattainable change your goal to suit the situation or change your approach. If at first you don't succeed, don't wait for others to change but change your own behaviour, create new avenues and try again.

3. If there's nothing you can do about the situation, then there's no need to attempt to control it so surrender to the situation. Don't attempt to swim against the current when it's strongest, let go and go with the flow. Making a conscious choice to accept the situation in itself is giving yourself a sense of control as you are the one that has made this decision, and you are dictating how you react to the situation.

The way you think effects the way you feel, and the way you feel influences your behaviour and experiences. It is a cycle that you can get stuck in or addicted to.

Some addictive drugs will illicit the release of feel good chemicals, similarly, all your emotions can be addictive too.

An emotion is nothing more than chemical release within the body that make you feel a certain way. Whether the chemical released within you creates a positive feeling or a negative feeling, the fact is that if it's released frequently enough by the same stimuli, your body will eventually miss it, expect it and seek ways to cause it to be released, just like an addiction.

Definition of addiction: A compulsive physiological and psychological need for a habit-forming substance.

Stress is a common example. As you get older your life tends to become busier and more stressful. Stress can come in forms of one-off life events like an accident, bereavement or health crisis but it is the small daily stressors that build up throughout your day and create most of your stress because they happen most frequently. Within an average day, I'm sure you can list hundreds of things that add to your stress levels such as rush hour traffic, your children, money worries, job pressures, household chores and the miserable weather conditions. These 'little' stressors cause the most suffering and yet, they are also the ones you have most control over in terms of how you respond, react and think about them.

Anxiety, butterflies in your stomach, lack of concentration, nervousness and all those other nasty feelings associated with stress are all due to a chemical release within your body. Heroin happens to boost a user's dopamine levels whilst stress stimulates the release of the hormone cortisol. Whether it is taking heroin or having to get the kids dressed and to school on time, there is a chemical response which the body responds to and eventually, if triggered enough, the body will expect and want more of it. We can become unwittingly addicted to our emotions in the same way as a smoker becomes addicted to nicotine.

You could argue that drugs cause a physical dependency whilst addiction to stress is an emotional dependency; however, the mechanism of becoming addicted is the same. For example, if you are frequently angry and have learnt to deal with most emotionally challenging situations by being angry, then you are already showing physical symptoms of emotional and physical addiction. How many times have you come home in a bad mood 'looking' for a row with your partner? Your partner does not need to have done anything wrong but you have consciously or unconsciously looked for something to create the argument. Being agitated, having that butterfly, knotted or wound up feeling inside are all examples (in this case) of the physical withdrawal symptoms from the biochemical's most frequently released from your endocrine system.

Over the years your body learns an internal biochemical response to an external event or stimulus. Eventually it will expect the internal feeling and if it does not appear it will send signals back up to the brain to search for what it 'needs'.

For example: A client of mine was worrying and anxious all the time. Her life was not particularly hard or unusually stressful but she could not stop feeling worried. She would worry about her health, her mortality, the future and her family. She could not understand why or when she had become a worrier but she did recognise that it was begin to become a significant problem in her life and was effecting her happiness.

As we worked together it quickly became clear that she had triggered the internal biochemical associated with anxiety and worry through her thoughts, and her body had become addicted to it. Initially my clients' thoughts would have wandered, causing various feelings but over time she started to pay attention to the worrying thoughts above all others. The worrying thoughts obviously set off a set of emotional responses that, in turn, made her feel anxious and more worried. This internal response then fed back to confirm the fact that she had things to be worried about and her brain said: *"see, I told you that you should be worried, look what you have found to worry about"*

This confirmation within my clients mind reinforced her worrying thought process because, what you focus on grows.

Like any rehearsed thought or brain function, the more you practise it, the more likely it will happen again. My client had become addicted to worry to the point where if she was not worried her body would miss the chemical emotion and her brain would ask where it's fix was. Her brain duly responded by searching for a worrying thought to provide the emotional 'hit'. This kept her stuck in the same cycle and experiencing the same emotional response to life. She had 'taught' herself to find something to worry about even when she was not worried. In effect, she was worried about not being worried!

I guarantee that you are addicted to your own emotions too. Whether it is stress, falling in love, being angry, being depressed or whatever emotional state it may be, your thoughts create feelings and feelings create your view of the world. You create your own reality by the way you think and subsequently feel about things.

"Your worst enemy cannot harm you as much as your own unguarded thoughts. A well-directed mind creates more happiness than even the love of your parents."

Buddha Shakyamuni

Recognising and changing the negative thoughts and feelings you are addicted to is a fundamental start to making your life happier and healthier.

HOME: POSITIVITY CREATES
HIGH HAPPINESS INCOME

"I am a scientist, not a Marketer. I chose my words very carefully. My claims are evidence-based. I have more than twenty years of on-the-job training in honing down my words to prevent overstatements. But from here, surveying the landscape of the latest scientific evidence for the build-effect, I say with confidence: positivity can change your life"
Dr Barbara Fredrickson in Positivity

THE THOUGHTS THAT YOU revisit time and time again are so ingrained and so hard-wired into your brain that they end up controlling your view of life and the feelings you hold about the world.

This is the negative thought-feeling cycle.

With such mental dedication and focus spent unconsciously seeking out all the little upsets that occurred in our day to get the chemical fix, we miss most of the good things that happen. If nothing negative happens for a while then the body will crave the negative hormones/chemicals and subsequently tell the mind to search its memory stores for some negative experience to create the associated thoughts and feelings. This is what psychology calls conditioning. Conditioning is a learned cause and effect response that we can unwittingly teach to ourselves.

Negative conditioning restricts your personal growth, it narrows your options in life and it reduces your choices.

Barbara Fredrickson has been studying positivity and positive emotions for over ten years and her research has been recognised with numerous honours. Dr Fredrickson points out the prehistoric need for negative emotions for our survival. The negative emotion of fear narrows our focus into the fight or flight mode. When faced with a threat, the negative emotions would drive us to either attack the posing threat or run away. In modern times, negative emotions such as stress are more common and yet the end result of narrowing our options is the same. With negative emotions our worldview and choices are significantly reduced leaving us little room to develop by narrowing our choices and our ability to grow. Extreme levels of negative emotions can incapacitate us into a state where we see no options or choices. We become engulfed with a sense of helplessness.

Positive emotions on the other hand do the opposite. Positive emotions significantly increase your worldview, broaden your possibilities and choices. Positive emotions help build your development, your skills and your strengths. Negative emotions narrow and stall whilst positive emotions broaden and build.

Positivity has far more benefits then negativity because it provides you with the means to achieve more, become more successful, develop your skills, strengths and your talents. Positivity even supports longevity through the process of broadening and building our choices and recourses.[59]

Dr Fredrickson's research has identified the ratio of positive-to-negative emotions needed to achieve a life full of purpose, meaning, well-being and growth. This ratio is 3:1.

That is to say, for every negative emotion you experience you should experience three or more positive emotions in order to flourish. Depressed individuals will typically have a positivity ratio of below one and therefore, their options will seem very narrow as negativity dominates their emotions. Anyone holding a positive-to-negative ratio of below 3:1 - i.e. three positive emotions to every one negative emotion - is at risk of negativity pulling them downwards. To flourish in life, you should take note of all the research laid out in this book and implement the techniques cited to increase your positivity score so that you attain a ratio of 3:1 or higher. Having three or more positive emotions for every single negative one will help override the downward pull of negativity and counteract its narrowing and stalling effect.

Take action to increase your positive emotions so that you enter into an upward spiral and enable the broadening and building effect of positivity.[35, 59] The techniques provided in this chapter will significantly help increase positivity and help you reach, or exceed your 3:1 positive-to-negative ratio, sending your positive emotions on an upwards trajectory.

WRITE A POSITIVE JOURNAL

Research shows that the simple act of writing a regular positive journal can bring you much income of happiness.[21, 22]

Each morning before you get started on your day, or each evening before you head off into a land of slumber, write your positive journal.

If writing your journal in the morning, describe all those things that you are looking forward to in your day ahead. Describe the positive people you are likely to meet, the achievements you are likely to make, the experiences you are likely to have. You can of course also refer and confirm the positive happenings you thought would arise during your previous day too.

If you are writing in the evening, then you can reflect on your day and recollect all the positive experiences you've had and anticipate all the positive things you are going to enjoy the following day.

It's simple and yet an extremely cost effective addition to your Business Plan for Happiness.

Not only does positivity bring you more life satisfaction and significantly boost your daily income of happiness but it will also increase your life expectancy.

There are so many variables at play when attempting to determine why some people live longer than others. Smoking, excess alcohol and other lifestyle factors such as living conditions and the amount of physical activity you do will all play a significant role in determining how long you live.[45, 118]

A study of nuns living in a nunnery was met with great excitement in the psychological community because nuns live very similar lives to one another, which means life variables were significantly reduced. They eat the same food, have the same health care, get the same amount of physical activity and virtually all lifestyle factors are the same.

The nuns all kept a daily diary and after several years these diaries were analysed. Taking all other factors into account, there was one determining factor that predicted how long they would live, which was the daily amount of positivity each expressed. Follow up research backs these initial findings and indicates that the positive effect of having a positive attitude and outlook can increase your life expectancy by as much as nineteen percent[109] or around ten years.[39, 95]

CALCULATE YOUR OWN POSITIVE TO NEGATIVE RATIO

To know how much you need to increase your upward happiness spiral, it is helpful to know where you are starting from. This is merely so you can track your progress. If you have a low score then you have a great opportunity for improvement.

Calculate your Positive to Negative Ratio. Visit: ***www.positivityratio.com***

Can you think of a time when, despite your life going well, there was still a niggling feeling within you that eventually overrode the good feelings? Before long you start to remember that you have not quite got everything you want and in fact, although things are going well, you are still a long way away from where you would like to be. You remember that you have something coming up in the future which will be stressful. You remember that you have not got the job you really want, the relationship you desire or the money you deserve and there you are once again, feeling more negative than positive, forgetting that life is actually going well for you.

You may enjoy friends and family but still you tend to create an underlying negative tone or 'colour' to your life, which for the most part, you are not aware of. All you know is that you are not as happy as you feel you should be. Unwittingly, you can be pulled down the negative spiral and become an expert in finding every little bit of negativity in your day to feed your negative addiction.

You leave the house in the morning and forget the car key. Innocent mistake though it is, without hesitation and as an instant reflex you make a tutting sound and say: *"typical!"* as if this minor forgetful action was "typical" of life's joke on you. Forgetting your keys is not seen as a simple act of forgetfulness but rather as another example of how you are at the cruel end of life. As if life is picking on you. You drop your mobile phone and say: *"typical!"* You are late for work and say: *"typical!"*

It rains just as you leave the house: *"typical!"* The traffic lights turn red: *"typical!"* You forget to get some money out of the bank before trying to pay for something in a shop: "typical!" Trip up the stairs and say: *"typical!"* Scratch the car; "typical!" Lose work on the computer: *"typical! Typical! TYPCIAL!"* You actively notice and even seek out every minute thing in your day that is not perfect and view them all as a personal vendetta against you.

In reality these types of things happen every single day to most people, all over the world. They are not special to you alone. They are not a result of life's sick sense of humour but merely examples of the unpredictable nature of life and the nature of humans. That is what makes life exciting isn't it? It is an unpredictable adventure. Who knows what magic each day will bring?

We can develop a conditioned tendency to focus on those little, insignificant hurdles. Hurdles that positive people would not even notice or pay a second thought to.

How you view the gauntlet makes all the difference between a broad, open, exciting, challenging and fulfilling life of opportunities and experiences, to one narrowed and stunted through negativity full of trepidation and fear.

When you face challenges in life (which you will), you have a simple choice. You can compound the challenge by narrowing and stalling your options through the development of anger, frustration and other negative emotions, and still have the problem. Alternatively, you can decide to let the negative emotions go, view the challenge with a positive mind and create positive emotions whilst dealing with the problem with a broader outlook. Either way, you will still have to face the challenge, the choice is to decide what feelings would you prefer to have and what would be most helpful for dealing with the problem?

Having a positive mind frame has huge implications on your health, wealth, relationships, productivity at work, creativity and resilience when times are hard.[51, 57] Training yourself to think more positively throughout everyday and in every situation is likely to be your bread-and-butter and is certainly capable of providing you with a stable and steady income of happiness.

Like all major accomplishments in business it can take hours of preparation, thoughtfulness, mindfulness and application but once the hard work is done and the contract is signed, the rest is plain sailing. The rewards and income of happiness gained from having an optimistic and positive mindset are more than worth the initial effort of being conscious of your own daily thoughts and feelings.

There is a statistical research method called Meta-analysis that involves researchers adding together the results of many studies on the same subject to get a larger sample. Researchers run statistical analysis on the collective results from all the studies to gain a more conclusive answer on the subject matter. A Meta-analysis was carried out on studies investigating the effects positivity has on success. The collective studies totalled experiments on over 275,000 people and Meta-analysis showed that regardless of other factors such as marriage, financial earnings or health, the one thing that made the most difference towards a successful life was the amount of positive emotions they experienced.[88]

To be clear, simply saying positive things when you really want to rant about a situation is not part of this Business Plan for Happiness and will bring you little or no happiness income. You need to create the correct internal state of feelings that will make it real.

VISUALISE YOUR BEST SELF

You must sincerely and whole heartedly feel the positivity within you by visualising how you would be as a very positive person. See what you would see, hear what you would hear and feel how you would feel. How would you stand, walk, talk and behave? Research suggests that this actually creates a positive response within you and your self-efficacy will increase as a result. i.e. you will begin to believe you are positive and will act like your positive visualisation of yourself.[89, 111]

When things do not quite go to plan you can always just carry on; being mindful of any negative thoughts that creep into your head and calmly ignore them. You can re-frame negative thoughts into positive ones or choose to listen to the bright, happy thoughts in your head instead.

When you forget your keys in the morning, you can chuckle, turn around and go back and get them. Simple. Not *'typical!'* Not a disaster. Not life trying to get at you. It is nothing but a simple mishap which is so easily rectifiable that it should not even pop up on your thought radar. If it rains when you leave the house perhaps think how nice it is not to have to water the garden or, if you are feeling particularly holistic, you may wish to stand there for a second or two and feel the refreshing rain on your face giving thanks for the life it gives. You can then carry on with your day taking positive feelings with you. When traffic is bad, you remind yourself that there is nothing you can do about it, so instead of getting frustrated or wound up, you can choose to do the opposite and relax, look around, marvel at the wonder of life and enjoy the positive feelings of being alive. This reframing is especially poignant if the traffic hold up is due to an accident. In such situations, you might choose to become conscious of the fact that, even though you may have been inconvenienced, there are others who are in a far worse situation in the accident ahead. Use the situation to be thankful for life and feel deep compassion for others who are less fortunate. As for forgetting to get money out of the bank, scratching the car, or whatever little mishap occurs during the day, try not to think about it at all. With such small happenings, accept them for what they are: nothing more than an insignificant, miniscule inconvenience that happens to people all over the world all of the time. On the grand scheme of life on earth, such small things are not worth thinking about so relax with a deep breath, smile and carry on regardless.

THE A.I.M APPROACH

Another helpful technique to create a more positive mindset is what Diener and Biswas-Denier (2008) call the "AIM approach" which is an anagram for the following steps:

- **A**ttention: We have already covered this approach whilst discussing our own efforts to ignore the minor "typical!" niggles within our day and choose to pay attention to all the marvellous wonders instead. You have a choice whether to pay attention to an ugly world or a beautiful world.
- **I**nterpretation: How many times have we made leaping judgements on people whilst knowing very little about them? How many times have we agreed with others after hearing only one side of the story?
- Have you ever accused someone of something knowing only a small part of the real situation? We have a tendency to fill in the missing pieces without the evidence. We tend to leap to conclusions without knowing the facts. Next time you see a car parked at a ridiculous angle making the free space next to it impossible to park in, do you assume that they have parked in that position and curse them for their inconsiderate parking or do you stop yourself from such thoughts and think that perhaps they were forced to park at an angle because of the angle of the car that was originally parked in the now unoccupied space? Check your interpretations; be careful not to jump to negative conclusions.
- **M**emory: Evidence consistently shows that spending time reminiscing and savouring past positive moments is beneficial to well-being and complements a positive frame of mind.

With a little bit of mindfulness towards your own thoughts and subsequent emotions throughout the day you can create a more positive and happier existence for yourself.

Reframe your own negative thought cycles into positive ones, pay attention to the positive things in your life and turn away from the negatives. With a change in focus of thought and mindset, the small hiccups and hurdles you meet will fade into the background and all the good, fun, lovely, thankful, beautiful, kind, caring, considerate, thoughtful, pleasant, enjoyable and exciting stuff that happens to you every single day has its volume turned up to FULL BLAST!

Recognise and prevent yourself from jumping to conclusions, interpret events positively and spend some time remembering and recalling past times that have made you happy.

Welcome to the cause side of life!

HOME: NEGATIVE MEDIA

"The media's the most powerful entity on earth. They have the power to make the innocent guilty and to make the guilty innocent, and that's power. Because they control the minds of the masses."
Malcolm X

THE NEWS WILL VERY rarely tell you anything positive and therefore can influence, or even sabotage your Business Plan for Happiness. If it is raining, the media reports on floods, traffic problems and the gloomy forecast. One particularly wet English summer, I even saw this headline:

The media can be very influential on our thoughts and to suggest that we "will be" depressed, even if meant as a tongue-in-cheek comment, was irresponsible. Be careful what news you tune into.

A few years ago, it snowed so heavily that most people were unable to get to work for a couple of days and schools were closed. To take advantage of the impromptu day off, everyone headed to the surrounding hills to go sledging. Neighbours and their families emerged from their homes pulling sledges or carrying random bits of materials that would slide on the snow. It was like a mass exodus and as if someone had made it compulsory to have fun that day. All the surrounding hills were dotted with similar scenes and entire communities were sledging, making snowmen and laughing as they ran away from snowball assaults.

How rare and special it was to see communities joined together with the sole purpose to have fun and play, and yet, the national newspaper headline read: *"WORST WHEATHER IN 50 YEARS!"*

Editors and reporters will continue to see it as their job to deliver tragedy, fear and negativity into every home if we continue to pay them for it. The financial reward from our pocket is so high that national newspapers have even been caught hacking into the phones of murdered children to get a scoop. They will pay someone tens of thousands of pounds for 'kiss and tell' stories with little consideration for the effect it will have on the implicated families and relationships because we pay for it.

Wouldn't it be nice to hear about the positive things that happen in the world?

It would be a refreshing change to read about the good things that are happening around the world, rather than page after page of doom and gloom. It would be inspiring to read a paper that told you about the kind actions of other people rather than murders and madness. We should be encouraging stories about the thousands of projects working to unite communities, reduce prejudices and bring people together. It would support your Business Plan for Happiness if you regularly received news about all the good, virtuous, kind, magical, amazing, beautiful and compassionate things being done around the world.

Far from being a wishy-washy optimist who wishes to bury our head in the sand and hide from the bad and sad things that happen, the reality is that we know extreme weather conditions cause havoc on the roads, rivers to swell and floods can cause great distress. This is not news. What would be interesting to know is how these people are being helped and supported by other people. Equally, like anyone who has heard anything about war, we know people will die but do we need to read about the inner details of how it happens?

We know that war causes great physical, emotional and psychological harm to individuals, families and nations. What about the support workers that are helping these people, what about the peace and trust that is being forged despite the war?

We also know that some people have psychological issues and that in extremely rare cases people with mental health problems commit terrible crimes. Fortunately it is rare but it does happen. We know these psychologically broken people exist but how does publishing articles and reports about them and the atrocities they commit benefit the nation?

We also know that, due to extreme views or misguided beliefs, some people do not consider anyone else's point of view and this causes community divide, racism and extremist behaviour. However, how does knowing more about extremism benefit our life? We all know extremism exists, what else do we need to know?

Be mindful of what you choose to read and focus on in the news because what you focus on grows.

"The news media are, for the most part, the bringers of bad news... and it's not entirely the media's fault, bad news gets higher ratings and sells more papers than good news."
Peter McWilliams

You could say if we do not read about the atrocities and tragedies then we cannot do anything about it. Knowing about deforestation may inspire a person to feel compelled to do something about it and support projects aimed at protecting the Planet. However, this person is just as likely to become inspired and take positive action if he/she read about existing projects that were already doing great things to prevent deforestation.

Charities tend to get the balance of information right. Charity adverts and events will usually spend more time and detail on what they are doing to resolve the issues rather than the problem.

Receiving regular information about the tragedy and suffering that restricts people's lives, causes of despair, heartbreak and loss will not prevent anything similar happening in the future but can create a negative thought-feeling cycle within a nation. It would be more effective as a preventative strategy to receive information about the amazing feats of human resilience, optimism, success, kindness, compassion, support and connection between mankind.

Negative news perpetuates negative news. Ironically, newspaper articles and news reports that present badness and sadness will inadvertently support the very thing they report on.

Reporting on terrorist actions, foiled terrorist plots and posting pictures of captured terrorists will not reduce terrorism but it may fuel it. Does the information in newspapers help unite religions and connect humanity or does it help to continue to separate us? Does endless reports on the tragic outcome of war help reduce the conflict or cause more terror rather than freedom?

Dramatic news stories tell us how we are in the worst recession for decades and how deep the recession is. Does this information help people feel confident to spend money and stimulate the economy or is it more likely to cause investors to pull their money out of the stock market, reduce trade and increase unemployment?

Be careful how much negative news you attend to and expose yourself to because it can influence your positive to negative emotion ratio in a negative direction.

TAKE ACTION:

"The media's power is frail. Without the people's support, it can be shut off with the ease of turning a light switch."
Corazon Aquino

A: Every time you go to buy a newspaper, read the headline first and think whether you really need to know more about it. How will knowing more enhance your life?

B: Subscribe to POSITIVE NEWS (*www.positivenews.org.uk*). This newspaper is how all newspapers should be. It's full of all the positive things that are happening all over the world. POSITIVE NEWS provides information about community cohesion projects, people working together to make a difference in the world. It reports on war, not as a means to underline the devastation it causes (that's obvious and not news), POSITIVE NEWS reports on the changes people in war torn countries are making to help reduce the suffering. POSITIVE NEWS reports on all the positive Government decisions and those Governments who are doing things radically different to help support life. POSITIVE NEWS highlights the amazing stories of human endeavour and achievement, it informs you about flourishing wildlife and the positive outcomes created through the efforts to support our planet and all those living on it.

C: Spread the word. Follow POSITIVE NEWS on Facebook and Twitter so that others can share the good news too. Your sharing will help start a new wave of positivity and, given what we know about the influence of media on Government, War, public opinion as well as our beliefs and behaviours, more newspapers like POSITIVE NEWS could really help change the world for the better. There is no doubt it will certainly help increase your level of happiness and positivity.

HOME: YOU CREATE
YOUR OWN REALITY

"Choose to take control of your own life. If you don't someone else will."
Unknown

IN THE 1890S A Russian called Ivan Pavlov set up an experiment to investigate the behaviour of a dog's natural salivary functions when feeding. Pavlov began by bringing out food for the dog causing it to salivate. Pavlov then started ringing a bell every time the food was brought out and once again, as you would expect, the dog produced saliva at the sight of the meal. After a while, Pavlov continued to ring the bell without presenting any food. Pavlov discovered that even though the dog could not see or smell the food, it continued to produce just as much saliva as if the food was presented. This experiment indicated that the dog's brain had made a mental link or association between getting fed and the sound of a bell. The dogs' physical body had learnt to react involuntarily (internal reaction of producing saliva) to the sound of a bell (external stimulus), even though there was no food around to smell, see or taste.

This experiment has been replicated in many different ways (including with humans) and all of these studies seem to show the same thing. Each experiment shows that our brain learns to associate or relate to certain stimuli, which causes involuntary, internal responses. In other words our brain learns to tell our body to react in specific ways due to what we have experienced and what thoughts and feelings we link to that experience.

This type of learning can help explain some of the strange behaviours we humans sometimes exhibit. Psychologists have developed and use a model called *Cognitive Behavioural Therapy* (CBT). I'm simplifying it hugely so I apologise to CBT experts but essentially, this therapy is based entirely around the way we learn or condition ourselves to behave in certain situations or when seeing or hearing certain things.

A thought creates a feeling, the feeling creates a physical response, which creates a behaviour. This is one of the ways you learn how to interact with the world, how you behave in certain situations, what you believe and how you feel about things.

Whether you avoid certain situations or are attracted to them can be based on this cycle. In fact, learned behaviours can develop from a behaviour or a thought but not with a feeling or physical response. Something has to precede the stimulation to release the hormones and biochemical's that create feelings and physical responses. The cycle has to start with either a thought or behaviour.

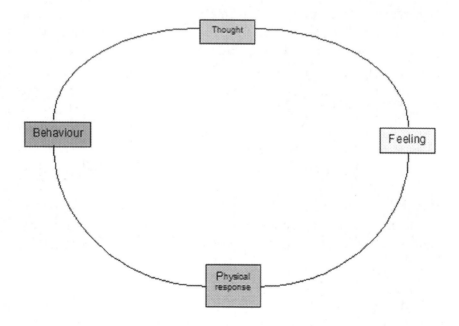

This type of learning goes on in every one most of the time. Throughout your life you have unconsciously collected millions of experiences and each one produced a thought, leading to an emotional feeling, which results in your behaviour (voluntary and involuntary, conscious and unconscious).

Imagine an untouched field of grass and a person walking through the centre creating a slightly visible path of flattened grass. When the next person comes across this field they are more likely to follow the same path, thus, making it even more visible and even more likely to be walked again and again. Like the stimulus–thought–behaviour link within our brain, the more the path is walked the more likely it is to be traversed in the future. I.e. the more you think and act in a certain way the more likely you are to produce the same behaviour again and again.

If you end up recalling the same negative thoughts and feelings repeatedly, you will learn to think, feel and behave in the same way over and over.

You can also see how thoughts and feelings can colour the way you think of yourself and who you are as a person and individual.

"I am not confident", "I am shy", "I am a clumsy person" etc.

Support your Business Plan for Happiness by recognising how powerful your mind is. Realise that any self-doubt, lack of confidence, low self-esteem or any limiting beliefs you may have about yourself are merely a product of your negative experiences that you mistake for yourself. You are not who you *think* you are.

Who you think you are now and what you think you can achieve in life is more limited then when you were born. You were free from negativities before being moulded by your mind. It is this false, illusionary self that we know as the Ego, but I shall refer to it as *mind-created-self* because it is a creation of the mind, a fabrication made up of experiences and not who you really are.

Through negativity you teach yourself to attract the thing you do not want. You attract people and situations that continue to make you feel down or negative about yourself. Whether it is a big capital 'NEGATIVE', or a small, niggling 'negative'; either way, it is still negative so change it today.

A point of reassurance is the fact that this model of learning is only part of the story. History tells us that in times of adversity, we humans have the ability to not only overcome but also adapt and rise to the challenges of life. We are not solely governed by the thought-feeling-behaviour model, we a have conscious choice.

Pavlov's salivating dogs experiment started a new paradigm of psychology called Behaviourism. Behaviourists believe that we are the sum total of our learned experiences. Behaviourists believe that we are governed and controlled by the thought-feelings-behaviour cycle. They believed that our behaviours are determined by the negative or positive reinforcement we experience throughout our life. Behaviourists would postulate that the desire to earn more money is the creation of the positive reinforcement we receive from the attainment of material possessions. The want to study is reinforced by the relief experienced once we have achieved our educational qualification. Depression could be linked to the negative experiences that reinforce listlessness, lack of motivation and encourage low mood. Pure Behaviourists believe that we are all at the mercy of the effect side of life.

It is true that your behaviour can be reinforced by your experiences and these experiences can mould your perception of self. However, Behaviourists do not account for one major factor: personal choice. You can be on the cause side and break the cycle if you choose to.

Psychologists Martin Seligman and Steve Maier assisted on an experiment designed to create behaviour in dogs through the negative reinforcement of small electric shocks. One group of dogs were given a simple way to avoid the electric shock by jumping over a small barrier whereas another group of dogs would receive shocks on both sides of the barrier. True to Behaviourism theory, the first group of dogs very quickly learned to jump any barrier as a natural response to their past experiences. The second group of dogs quickly learned that there was no way to stop the shocks and learned to give up trying. Even if their situation changed and the experimenters gave the dogs an opportunity to escape from their negative experience these dogs did not attempt to look because their past experience had told them that there was no escape and therefore, no point trying. They had learned to be helpless.

However, a small handful of dogs never gave up, they continued to search for a way out even though they were in the same situation as the helpless dogs. This show of conscious will and barefaced resilience in the face of adversity turned the long-standing model held by Behaviourists on its head. This experiment suggested that our behaviours were not exclusively determined as the result of the cause and effect of our experiences. Now there seemed to be a new psychological view, one that incorporated conscious choice and free will.[1] Some dogs gave up in the belief that their situation will never change whilst other dogs seemed to make a choice to never stop trying to improve their situation.

Psychologists began to wonder if humans had the same option of free will or learned helplessness in life. Do some people have a negative experience and decide to give up trying anything like it again and are there other people who never quit trying regardless what their past experiences were like?

To answer these questions Donald Hiroto from Oregan State University conducted an experiment on humans.[73] Hiroto assembled two groups of individuals. Group A were put into a room where an annoying and continuous sound was introduced. This group could stop the noise by pressing a specific sequence of buttons. Group B were put in the same situation but no sequence of button pressing would switch off the noise.

After this initial stage of the experiment both groups were introduced to a different room where they were subjected to a completely different sound and a different method of turning off the noise. This time however, both Group A *and* Group B had the opportunity and ability to find a way to switch off the noise.

As predicted, and inline with the Behaviourist model, Group A transferred and generalised their learned behaviour from their experience at stage one of the experiment and within seconds found the correct method to stop the new irritating noise (by touching one side of the room and then the other). However, in line with Maier and Seligman's work, most of Group B transferred their knowledge from stage one of the experiment and did not attempt to find an escape from the noise. Even though it was a different situation and a different noise, Group B had made a conscious decision to give up and endure the irritating sound. Based on their past experiences, this group had decided that there was no point trying and that their efforts would amount to nothing.

What was even more intriguing, however, was that some participants in Group B never gave up trying to find relief from the noise in both first and second stages of the experiment. Despite their experience in stage one, where their attempts to stop the noise were futile, they remained resilient in stage two and continually put effort in to find a way out of the noisy situation. Their resilience was rewarded by finding the correct way to turn off the noise in the second stage of the experiment.

From their experiments and many others that followed, Maier, Seligman and Hiroto had effectively discovered pessimism and optimism.

These key findings showed that your behaviour is not a product of your experiences alone. You are not a robot governed solely by the stimulus-response effect of your experiences, you have a choice to either give up or keep going. Keep striving forwards and never give up. You have a choice to be a pessimist or an optimist.

To be an optimist, start by being more aware of how you are feeling and what you are thinking, then turn any negative or pessimistic thoughts into a positive. Be mindful, be persistent and be patient in the knowledge that, as a pessimist, you will give up trying even when the solution could be right in front of you. Never give up on your dreams because you never know how close you are.

It takes a very special type of person to decide to stop thinking and feeling a certain way without some degree of effort. You need to be patient and practise changing your thoughts throughout each and every day from here onwards until you naturally and unconsciously seek out positive thoughts, feelings and behaviours. Replace your negative addiction to release hormones that make you feel great, sexy, beautiful, likeable, chilled out, relaxed, considerate or just plain good about yourself.

If you have learned an exercise, a lifting technique, dance or martial arts move incorrectly it can take longer and many more repetitions to correct the movement. Similarly, once you have learned to think in a negative fashion, it will take more time and effort to unlearn it and change it into a positive habit of thought; although the effort is worth it.

If you have taught yourself to feel that life is working against you and that it is you against the world most of the time, then you are likely to attract exactly that. Pessimists are eight times more likely to suffer from depression after a tough time and suffer from ill health; they are eight times more likely to do less well at school, at work and in their social and personal lives. Pessimists are eight times more likely to live shorter lives than their optimistic brothers and sisters. If you would like to be healthier, have more life satisfaction and increase your chances of living a longer happier life, practise the practical applications of this book.

CHANGE YOUR MOODY SELF

To change your negative thought cycles into more positive ones you have two options:

1. You can change your thoughts by being more mindful and in control of them, or use the A.I.M approach, which will then affect the feelings you have and then affect your behaviour;
2. Change the way you are feeling by calling on friends and family or watching your favourite comedian on DVD. Do something to change your mood such as going for a walk somewhere nice, have a workout at the gym, enjoy a relaxing bath or meditate. Take action to lift your internal state because this feeds through the thought-feeling cycle helping you feel, behave and think more positively.

Now it is time to look at the three 'selves' of optimism.

1. Self-Confidence; the belief in your own ability.[36]
2. Self-Efficacy; your belief in your ability to reach your goals.[10]
3. Self-Reflection; arguably the most important of the three in terms of being motivated to reach your goals. Self-Regulation is linked to Self-Efficacy.

Self-Reflection is very important in your progress to become more positive and motivated to reach your desired goals in life. Self-Reflection incorporates both Self-Confidence and Self-Efficacy, which in turn, creates motivation. Therefore, without Self-Reflection the necessary internal states (e.g. motivation, confidence, desire etc.) will not arise. Whether you reach your desired goal or not is more determined by what you *believe* you can achieve rather than what you can actually do. You can test your abilities on any given task but ultimately, the true deciding factor whether or not you are successful is your Self-Reflection.

Put simply: If you believe you can't you probably can't. However, if you believe you can you probably can, regardless of what your previous experience may tell you.

If you believe in yourself there is little you cannot achieve no matter what academic tests may say. If you regard yourself as highly efficacious and have strong determination and belief in yourself, you will act, think and feel as if you can; whereas if you are unsure, you will cautiously approach your goal with mild motivation and aspiration.

CHALLENGE YOUR NEGATIVE SELF

When an issue arises in your life and you recognise that your mind-created-self is filling your day with negative, pessimistic thoughts, follow these steps to help challenge them:

- What specifically caused your negativity?
- What do you believe about your situation that creates your negative outlook?
- Are your beliefs founded on absolute fact? What could be an alternative belief? If your negative thoughts are caused by someone else, what might their viewpoint be? Why might their mind-created-self cause them to behave that way?
- Your situation will teach you some positive learnings to help you grow, what could those learnings be? i.e. To be patient. To confirm the negative effects of our mind-created-self and the pointlessness of negative emotions like anger. To reassess what really matters in life. To understand others more To have more compassion. To give you an opportunity to practise some of your happiness income techniques. Every obstacle is an opportunity to help you learn, be better and develop.
- Recognise that your situation is not personal, it's not life picking on you and it's within your own control to view the situation differently. Notice the strengths you already have to deal with the situation and the learning opportunities it will provide you with.

You have the power to create your own future through positivity and Self-Reflection. Be an optimist and believe in yourself.

There is a big difference between saying positive statements and believing them so combine your words with visualisations or a behaviour that initiates a positive physical response to create the appropriate positive feelings. By triggering a positive physical feeling within you, any affirmations you say become consciously and unconsciously connected with the related positive feeling and this becomes your positive thought-feeling cycle. With regular practise and mindfulness this becomes your new learned response to challenging situations.

USE A MANTRA EFFECTIVELY

Take your mind back to a time when you were completely *[relaxed]*, *[happy]*, *[contented]*, *[amazing]*, *[sexy]*, *[confident]*, see what you saw, hear what you heard and create all those positive feelings that you experienced at the time. Immerse yourself in the moment. Bring back any associated smells, feelings, sounds, colours and movement of your surroundings. Make it real and immerse yourself within the reminiscing by 'seeing' everything through your own minds-eye as if you were there now.

Once there, introduce and repeat your appropriate Mantra:

e.g. *"I am [relaxed], [happy], [contented], [amazing], [sexy], [confident] now"*

Notice the use of the word "now" in a mantra. It is important to include this in any mantra because your mind does not know the difference between reality and feelings. Your reality is a creation of your mind and if you recall past experiences vividly and in full sensory detail, as far as your mind is concerned your visualisations are real, which is why it triggers the appropriate feelings. You will already know this from your own experiences. There will be times when you have relived an event in your mind, replayed the situation as a mind-movie which would have triggered the feelings as if you were there. With this in mind, simply stating: *"I will be happy"* as a mantra will not trigger the feelings. You have to convince your mind that you are there (wherever you choose 'there' to be) already saying: *"I am happy now"* as you recall a happy time in detail. See what you saw, smell what you smelt, hear what you heard and feel those happy feelings now.

If the positive experience you recall is associated with a negative feeling, choose another time. It is the positive internal state (feeling), which your mind creates from your visualisation mantra that is important rather than the actual event you recall. For example, recalling a happy time with someone who is no longer with you may create feelings of sadness rather than happiness.

This sounds so simple and yet it really can have a profoundly positive influence on your own Self-Efficacy.[89] Your mind is a powerful tool at your disposal so use it to recall how you want to feel. Create positive images and play positive mind-movies of times that will allow you to see, hear and feel how you want to project yourself now, because perception is projection.

CREATE YOUR MANIFESTATION BOARD

To keep your mind focused on what you want to achieve in life, how you want to be and to keep yourself fuelled with positive feelings about you and your future, it can be very useful to create a manifestation board. This board should depict all the things you want in your life, all the things that you would like to see yourself achieving and doing and then see it and visualise it as if you already have it. Collect pictures, quotes, clippings or whatever you need to create your board as long as it means something to you.

Place your manifestation board up in a prominent place where you will see it regularly enough to take some time hoping, believing and getting excited about the true possibility that it will all come true. Once again, when thinking about your manifestation board use your imagination to view yourself and your life as if everything on your manifestation board is true and as if you have it all now. How would you feel? How would you think? How would you talk? How would you look? How would you behave?

Remember, this not only creates a very positive mindset which will reflect positivity on how you behave and feel, it will also keep your conscious and subconscious mind aligned and directed towards a positive future and you'll be amazed how your dreams begin to come true.

You can also choose to laugh for no reason (preferably on your own!). This will change your feelings and will feed positively into the thought cycle and potentially change your view accordingly. There are Laughter Workshops that are designed to do just this. You could also choose a behaviour that will make you think happy thoughts or feel happy like going to see a friend, watching your favourite comedian on DVD or better still, watch your favourite comedian with friends because the universal agreement is that having friends and family around is one of the most important components of happiness.[127]

Lasting happiness comes from within you so use your body's own natural chemical supply to create positive feelings through thought until this increased positivity naturally triggers positive emotions throughout your day and your base level of lasting happiness rises.

The more you counteract negative thoughts by replacing them with positive or happy ones, the more the nice feelings will take preference and override the negative. This optimistic positivity will become your new and natural thought-feeling-behaviour cycle.

How would you like to see the world? How would you like to see yourself? There is nothing that you cannot be if you believe it. Every man-made creation started with a single thought. Start to think positively and take action now. Be a pessimist and give up, or be an optimist and succeed? Make your decision right now.

HOME: UNDERSTANDING OTHERS

"We can never be truly free whilst another is in slavery."
Unknown

VIEWING OTHERS AS MORE important than your self will reduce the risk of falling into a negative spiral.

We tend to compare other people and their situation against our own situation. This comparison can work to our favour in a positive reframe by comparing upwards: e.g. *"I will be as content as you one day"* or downwards: e.g. *"I have so much to be thankful for in comparison to others."*

Whilst working with cancer patients, Kate Hefferon from the University of East London recognised that optimism was still present. [70] Some patients used downward and upward social comparisons to help reframe their situation into a positive thought cycle. When comparing themselves to patients that had already finished therapy they upwardly compared in a positive frame saying: *"One day that will be me"* Alternatively, patients will also compare themselves downwardly when looking at younger patients or patients with a more aggressive disease saying: *"At least I am older"* or *"At least mine is not as aggressive as others."*

No matter how tough your situation may be, you always have a choice to frame your thoughts positively, and appropriate social comparison can be a helpful way to do this.

There are two caveats to use when comparing yourself to others:

1: Your comparison must always be associated with positive emotions and compassion. Comparing yourself and your situation against other people is not an opportunity to feel superior or even pity other people, it is an opportunity to feel grateful for all the things you have in your life whilst feeling love and compassion for those less fortunate.

Additionally, you should not pity someone who acts upon the illusions of their mind-created-self but instead you should understand the cause of negativity and show patience. Remember, everyone is trying to increase their happiness using the resources thay have available to them. Their resources may be limited or severely damaging but nonetheless, they are still doing the best they know how with what they think will help bring them more happiness.

For example: if someone burgles your home, you will obviously be upset and feel negative emotions, which is natural. However, you could challenge any negative emotions and hurtful thoughts towards the burglar because you understand that they are working with a severely flawed happiness business plan. They have taken material possessions that are ultimately unimportant on the grand scale of life and they are unlikely to find true lasting happiness because they believe it comes from having more possessions. This thinking will enhance your compassion. Perhaps the thief has a drug or alcohol dependency and exchanges the goods he steals for a fleeting, momentary glimpse of drug-induced happiness (or numbness). If the burglar continues with his flawed happiness business plan, he will continue to be emotionally bankrupt and his futile search for lasting happiness will never end. This creates feelings of compassion within you.

Some problems cannot be changed but you have a choice to:

A) Have the problem and enter into a negative spiral of anger or hate.

B) Have the problem and enter into a positive lift of compassion and understanding.

There may be a part of you that pines for your lost possessions but it is such feelings of attachment that caused the thief to steal from you in the first place. You should feel compassion for the person who took your goods because you know they are suffering for the same reason that causes you to grasp at the goods they took. You feel sadness and compassion towards them in the knowledge that they are causing more suffering for themselves due their misconceived search for happiness within possessions rather than within themselves.

Your compassion comes with no feelings of superiority but from the sincere wish for everyone to be happy because it is what you ultimately want to.

2: Make all attempts to stop making any comparisons between your wealth and possession with other people. Research shows that beyond a certain point, the level of a nations happiness does not increase with the country's level of wealth[72] However, the inequality of wealth within communities or between the states in a country does matter, but not in a good way. The research suggests that when people compare their wealth with others within and around their geographical area, they are either happier or less happy depending on how they compare. If an individual is on a lower income than their neighbour, their happiness level will tend to be lower. This is reversed with the richer neighbour who will be happier when comparing themselves against their poorer neighbour.

Increasing your level of happiness by financial comparison is a fragile method to gain more happiness because you may be wealthier than your neighbour today but your level of happiness will drop if they earn more than you tomorrow. The research suggests that by comparing your level of income with other people in your peer, social or geographical group, you are consciously or unconsciously wishing that they remain less wealthy than you. This is contrary to the first caveat of social comparison.

Aspire to make money and buy nice things because you deserve them, like them and have fun doing it but do not rely on any of it for lasting happiness. Make every effort to retain positive compassion and avoid looking down on less fortunate people to make you happier.

With the right mindset and positivity, the 'life sorrows' you experience can help dispel your own self-grasping, destroy pride, help develop compassion and create virtuous actions. All of which will manifest a more peaceful, loving and happier life for your self.

These tools, techniques and frame of mind will be the beginning of true compassion and lasting happiness within your HOME.

REST: THE IMPORTANCE
OF MEDITATION

"Man is the strangest thing. He sacrifices his health in order to make money, then sacrifices his money to recuperate his health. This makes man so anxious about his future that he does not enjoy the present. He lives as if he is never going to die, and then dies having never really lived"
His Holiness The 14th Dalai Lama

A VERY POWERFUL WAY to quieten your negative mind-created-self is to meditate. You now know that positivity increases success and longevity through the broadening and building effect (Pg.35) and another way to increase your level of positivity is to meditate.[59, 60]

Until recently the concept of meditation would conjure up images of humming hippies floating in uncomfortable looking crossed-legged positions but nowadays the importance and benefits of meditation have become widely recognised by the mainstream and the good news is mindful meditation can be done in many ways.

You are receiving an unbelievable amount of information each waking second, which you cannot process all at once. To cope with the amount of information, your brain has to constantly work to filter out what it believes to be irrelevant or unimportant whilst choosing to focus on what it believes to be of use at that particular moment. Meditation helps improve this filtering system and deal more efficiently and effectively with what is important. This helps to significantly increase well-being through mechanisms such as reduced stress, increased focus and ability to cope.

Without meditation the mind never rests. It is constantly churning over thousands of thoughts, words, discussions and images every second. Even in your sleep, thoughts of the day seep into your dreams and you have nightmares or restless nights plagued by your relentlessly active mind.

Imagine driving in a car on a motorway at a hundred miles per hour with hundreds of other vehicles equally determined to get ahead of each other. Whilst you try to navigate your way through the whizzing traffic, your side passenger is tuning the radio in and out so that you are hearing snippets of radio stations followed by white noise. If this isn't enough to deal with, there is also a back seat passenger who constantly asks the obligatory question: *"Are we there yet? Are we there yet? Are we there yet…"*

Like the mass of information that hits your five senses every second of every waking hour, your noisy and chaotic motorway drive makes you easily distracted and hard for you to concentrate. You become highly pressured, stressed and highly likely to make a disastrous mistake.

This sort of chaotic bombardment of information and distractions are what you have become accustomed to in your everyday life. Your brain is constantly processing and filtering millions of stimuli and you can find even the simplest of tasks stressful as a result.

Now imagine that you are on the same motorway but this time everything is peaceful. The few cars that join you on the motorway are driving slowly and spread out at a safe distance. The radio is switched off and you have no passengers. This journey is quiet and you can easily concentrate. In this scenario your driving is relaxed, precise and efficient and you are far better equipped to deal with any potential emergency manoeuvre.

Just a few minutes of meditation each day can help you achieve this type of inner peace and focus. Meditation allows your mind to filter out all the rubbish and distracting chatter, allowing you to concentrate on the things that are important and necessary.

It is no wonder that regular practitioners of meditation have lower blood pressure. In fact, when compared to a control group, even novice meditators show significant reduction in hypertension.[107] In addition, people who meditate are less stressed and have less anxiety[52, 28] and meditators seem to have more protection against cognitive decline.[28]

In 2005 the World Bank began offering meditation classes to all ten thousand employees as part of a fifteen-year commitment to promote staff health. Containing forty-minute discussions and theory surrounding meditation followed by just twenty-minutes practical participation, surveys showed that employees reported feeling less stressed at work and at home. They felt more able to cope, felt happier, more focused and more productive. Out of all the health programmes that the company ran over the fifteen years, meditation classes were most frequently attended by executives and higher-ranking staff members' than any other programme, proving that meditation is not just for hippies.

Having said that, meditators may become more hippy-like which is great because research shows that meditators not only look happier[29] they are more likely to be focused and feel increased compassion and empathy which, as we know, also increases levels of happiness.[28]

Meditation helps train your mind to be less negative, less active and less chaotic allowing you to enjoy the present moment.

There is no set way to meditate but rather a matter of what suits you. The main priority during meditation is to re-train the mind to filter out distractions and unnecessary thoughts easily enabling it to function more effectively. You know the importance of resting every other muscle in your body so why not start resting the mind through meditation too?

Limit any distractions before starting any form of meditation practise. Switch off your mobile phones and any electrical equipment that may distract you. Choose a relatively quiet place and time where you are unlikely to be disturbed.

THE BASICS OF STARTING MEDITATION

There are several ways to meditate and several types of meditation, choosing one that suits you will require some research and practise of your own but for the purpose of getting you started, I will describe a basic breathing Meditation for you to replicate.

Sit on the floor or a chair as long as your back is straight. To ensure your back is straight, try and imagine that a piece of string running from your backside (fixing your backside to whatever it is you are sitting on) through your spine, all the way up your back to the neck, passing in between your ears and out of the crown of your head. Imagine now that this string is pulled tight at the top, lengthening and lifting your spine allowing all your bones and limbs to simply hang, comfortably, relaxed in a natural position with your shoulders back and head looking forward.

Once in this position you are ready to start practising being still in body and mind.

To help you do this, focus on a spot or object (perhaps a flower, candle or statue of a Buddha) a few feet in front of you. Relax your gaze rather than staring like you are attempting to fire lazars from your eyeballs. Once relaxed and in position, take your consciousness and move it to the very back of your skull. By this I mean, focus on taking thoughts from the front of your head and moving them backwards so that they sit up in the back. Think of it like moving yourself from the front of a cinema to the very back row. This will significantly help you focus.

Be gently mindful of keeping your consciousness on the back row of your skull throughout your meditation practice. I say 'gently' because as soon as you are beginning to engage in your meditation practice, everything you do should be graceful, nothing sudden, no 'aggressive' movements of thought, body or mind. If you notice your consciousness has moved to the frontal lobe, gently, calmly and gracefully, slide it back.

Now you have everything set to begin. You are seated with your limbs hanging softly off a straight spine and frame. Your consciousness is viewing the world from the back of your skull and your gaze is relaxed out to a few feet in front of you.

Continued...

Continued...

Now take a slow deep breath in this way: as you breathe in through your nose your lungs will fill, not by sniffing in air through your nose but by expanding your stomach.

As your stomach gently rises, notice how air is naturally drawn into your lungs with ease. Once your lungs are full, open your mouth slightly and simply, gently let go and the air will leave your lungs out through your mouth effortlessly as your stomach naturally relaxes back down towards your spine.

Continue this breathing pattern, gently and calmly until you feel ready to move onwards.

Once you feel your mind is suitably calmed, begin to move your consciousness with your breathing. As air is naturally pulled in through your nose, 'see it' being driven to the back of your head where your consciousness is resting. Perhaps it is helpful to imagine your consciousness being gently washed by the incoming air, like a fan has been switched on. The air washes your consciousness out the back and down through your head and out of your mouth as the stomach relaxes.

Continue this breathing pattern whilst also being gently aware of maintaining good posture, gentle focus and remaining relaxed. Do this at least once a day and for at least fifteen minutes.

N.B: Periodically keep check on your mind. Your thoughts should mostly be caught up in your breathing cycle but without checking, your mind-created-self can be very sneaky. If you don't keep checks you will find yourself drifting off to sleep or into a day-dream, neither of which will train your mind into an obedient super trained elite warrior.

It is important to have structure during your initial meditation practise because without keeping your mind-created-self occupied, it will chatter with questions and wander off frequently. There may be noises that distract you or the mind-created-self may deliberately try and sabotage your attempts to quieten it. Treat your interrupting mind like a child who does not want to do their homework. The child may protest, become easily distracted and find ways to divert attention away from the homework but as the adult, it is your role to be patient, remain calm and encourage the child (your mind) to settle and focus. During mediation view your mind like that child and yourself as the loving but determined parent.

When practising meditation it can help to confirm the fact that your mind-created-self is a separate thing from your real jewel-like-self. Notice how the mind chatters away while the real you waits patiently 'underneath'. Like observing someone else talking, the observer is the real you.

You should let go and calmly return to quietening your mind whenever your attention drifts away from your meditation. If you are counting, start back at the beginning; if you are focusing on your breathing, re-focus; and if you are trying to clear all thought simply observe any thoughts and calmly slide them back out of your mind.

To begin with, it is common to find that your mind seems more active when you meditate. This can be frustrating but practise patience and remember that your mind-created-self does not like being pushed aside, just like the child protesting against their homework or chores, but you have decided that from now on it is you who is in control and not your mind-created-self.

Studies show that on average people do not tend to experience increased levels of well-being until around the third week of regular meditation practise so bear this in mind when starting out.[60] It is extremely worthwhile sticking to your new meditation routine because after the third week you will experience a significant dose-response and the positive benefits in the form of positive emotions, happiness and well-being will increase three-fold. In other words, the same amount of time spent in meditative practise will bring in three times as much happiness income when compared to the previous three weeks.

When investigating the actual mechanisms that produce the benefits of meditation, Dr Fredrickson identified four specific areas, which are:

1. Increased ability to savour past, present and future more effectively.
2. Meditators gain improved and more positive sense of self. They accepted themselves and like themselves more.

3. Meditators find themselves enjoying other people more through better relationships, understanding and feelings towards others.
4. Mediators increase positive health behaviours and feel healthier. This reflects on their increased feelings of happiness.[60]

These benefits were equally pronounced in both individual and group meditation classes.[59]

Persevere with your meditation practise. Ten to fifteen minutes each day will eventually quieten your mind-created-self, like the child who eventually succumbs to the realisation that their protests and tantrums get no response.

You can also practise a type of meditation by savouring the moment when you are performing quiet chores or hobbies such as ironing, painting, walking, getting dressed, or eating.[123] All you have to do is purposefully pay attention to every little detail during your quiet activity whilst consciously filtering out any other thoughts that come into your mind. When ironing for example, notice your gentle breathing, notice how the iron feels in your hand, notice the way it glides across the fabric and how the fabric smoothes over. The more you practise clearing your mind and spend quiet time savouring the present moment the easier it will become and eventually it will happen automatically.

There are many types of meditation practise and the technique described is a good starting platform. Continue with this technique and after a month or more, begin investigating Transcendental Meditation, Mindfulness Meditation and Buddhist Meditation to increase your knowledge and expand your practise.

The benefits and inner journey you are able to reach through meditation should not be underestimated, and yet, on a very simplistic level, initial meditative practise should be essentially aimed at quietening and controlling your mind. Like a well-trained animal, meditation will enable you to perform any activity efficiently and precisely to the exclusion of any distractions. With this in mind you can begin by personalising your meditative sessions to suit you.

THE PRESENT MOMENT MEDITATION

Choose a time in your day when you have ten minutes to practise, experiencing the life that opens up in front of you within that moment.

When you find yourself in a relatively quiet moment within your day, if you are undisturbed for a while, take the time to practise this meditative exercise.

Perhaps you have ten minutes to sit on a park bench, washing the dishes, hanging clothes out on the washing line, running the bath, eating your lunch, walking to the shops, picking the children up from school, or whatever activity you find yourself doing, sink into the activity. Notice the details. Notice how things feel in your hands, beneath your feet and within your body. Recognise any sounds that are associated with the activity. Listen to all the other sounds around you too. Truly look at the world around you. Watch how things move. Notice how you move and interact with your environment. Look at the colour of things, how the colours change and how the light interacts with you and your surroundings.

Absorb the activity and your surroundings through every sense in your body and being so that you can teach and train your mind more frequently, preventing it from running off into the future and scheduling you in for all those other things you have to get done. At least once a day for just a few minutes, take timeout whilst engaged in an activity to pull on the reins of your mind and say: *"Easy now! Let's just hold up here for a while and really experience life, my surroundings and this moment in all its glory"*

This practise is to complement your main mediation practise rather than replace it, but either method is a good place to start bringing in some happiness income.

The western Taoist, Barefoot Doctor, describes a really nice and imaginative meditative practice in his book: *Handbook for the Urban Warrior,*[11] that is paraphrased here for your interest.

Once you have positioned yourself correctly and prepared yourself for meditation, start to concentrate on your breathing. Picture your spine as the face of a cliff and as your belly rises on inspiration, waves at the bottom of a cliff recede away before gently washing back in as you exhale. Spend time imagining the waves in your belly rolling in and out as you breathe. Hear the waves and the sound they make against the rock of the cliff, see it in your mind's eye, smell the fresh, crisp sea air and feel the spray carried in the breeze.

Immerse yourself in this imagery for a while and when you are ready, slowly float up the cliff face whilst noticing the moss and ferns clinging to all the nooks and crevasses. Notice the dampening sound of the waves below as you drift up your spine and up the cliff. Notice how the wind moves your hair and clothing. Spend time experiencing this journey through all your imaginary senses. When you eventually reach the area of your heart you will find a cave. Venturing into this cave the distant waves sound as if you have your ears to a shell. In the cave, sitting in a meditative lotus position you find a Buddha looking completely at peace. Feel the Buddha's peace as you watch. Once filled with the calm and contentment of the Buddha, without moving or changing the Buddha sends out a warm beam of compassionate light from his heart. The cave gets lighter as the Buddha's compassion and love spreads through you, out of the cave, out of your chest filling your body and your surroundings. Spend time enjoying the warmth of the Buddha's compassionate love within you.

This may work well for you or may be a phonetic or auditory version would suit you best? You can sit in a park meditating to the sound of the wind or by a river. You may wish to use one of the many meditative CDs that are available to buy. Whichever method suits you best in the beginning of your new meditation practise ensure that it focuses your mind on one thing or nothing at all.

During your early stages of practising meditation it can be helpful to keep your eyes closed to minimize distractions although you must stay awake. Eventually, when you feel that meditation is becoming easier and your mind-created-self surrenders and quietens more rapidly, you should begin meditating with your eyes open. Keeping your eyes slightly open during meditation will help to carry the inner focus and calm into your waking day.

When you reach a level where you have your eyes open it is recommended that you focus on something peaceful, beautiful or spiritual, like a flower, a picturesque landscape or a statue of a Buddha.

Setting time aside for meditative practise can be hard at first because western culture conditions you to feel guilty about taking time out for yourself. You often think that you have not the time because your mind-created-self is too busy listing all the things you have to do first. Before you know it, you have not meditated for weeks. Be conscious of this trap and once you have planned a set time to meditate do not change it. When your mind makes excuses to delay your meditation session, remember that you are the adult and it is the child. Recognise that this is exactly the reason why you need to take time out to meditate. Regular meditation will settle your disruptive childlike mind and is likely to result in you having more free time due to a more effective, efficient and productive mind.

With a small degree of patience and perseverance, meditation will very quickly become an activity that you will look forward to and you will notice huge physical, emotional and social benefits.

Meditation is an extremely powerful tool towards the pursuit of lasting happiness and evidence shows people who meditate regularly are far more positive about their lives[49] Meditation should be a priority and one of the initial target areas in your Business Plan to Happiness.

WORK: WHAT ROLE DOES
MONEY PLAY?

"Money will buy a bed but not sleep; books but not brains; food but not appetite; finery but not beauty; a house but not a home; medicine but not health; luxuries but not culture; amusements but not happiness."

Unknown

MONEY IS THE THING most likely to be cited as a means to increase happiness but money has nowhere near as much influence on levels of happiness as you may think.[5]

Coming into great wealth (winning the lottery for example) can actually decrease your level of lasting happiness in the long-term.[43, 81, 64] Lottery winners will find themselves happier initially but after a relatively short period they return back to the same level of happiness (or lower) as before their new found fortune. Reports from lottery winners also say that personal friendships become strained and worries and mistrust significantly increase which negatively affects their level of happiness.

Tal Ben-Shahar[12] postulates that the financially rich and wealthy can feel under increased pressure to be happy, after all, they are surrounded by all the material objects they could want so what reason can they have to be unhappy? For westerners who are less well off financially it is common to blame lack of happiness on lack of money. However, if they become very rich the research shows that they are likely to discover that having more money does not provide more happiness. This realisation can lead to despair and they become even less happy. The financially wealthy realise that they *should* be happier because they have everything that is believed (mostly by the western world) to provide happiness and yet they feel emotionally bankrupt.

It is interesting to know that despite our generation being far wealthier than in 1955, our level of happiness has changed little and we experience much higher amounts of anxiety and depression.[72]

For the average individual, the optimal financial income that provides increased and lasting happiness is around £3000 per month.[69]

Research suggests that having and maintaining a sense of control in your life is key to your level of happiness.[117] As income increases above £3000 per month your life choices, decisions and options also increase. Bank managers, accountants and financial advisors begin to provide you with plans, investments and share options, ultimately decreasing your sense of control. For a single person, an income of £3000 per month will provide increased choices without taking away your sense of control.

A financial income of £3000 per month also provides another crucial element to lasting happiness in terms of meaning. With too much money you can buy all you wish for at any given whim, which can take away a sense of meaning, sense of achievement and accomplishment.

This reminds me of a boy in my year at secondary school who came from a wealthy family and always had the latest gadgets, bikes, toys and clothes. I remember saying how wonderful it must be for him to have anything he asked for but he envied the fact that other classmates had paper-rounds or other part-time jobs to earn their money and save up for the things they wanted. It gave him no pleasure or sense of achievement to simply ask for what he wanted. On his birthday and at Christmas there was no sense of unknown or excitement because he knew he would get all the presents he wanted.

I like the saying: *Give your children enough to do something but not enough to do nothing.*

It is not true to say that money has no role in your Business Plan for Happiness. It is good to want nice things for yourself and for your family but material possessions are not to be seen as a means to gain happiness. Once your basic needs are met and you are comfortable, it is a much sounder happiness investment to give the excess cash away to a charity or spend it on someone else.[48, 96]

The search for happiness within material possessions is like drinking salty water to quench your thirst. The more you drink the thirstier you get. The more you search for contentment outside of yourself the further away from contentment you will be.

There are some people who will say that this does not apply to them because they arc financially rich and still very happy. Research clearly indicates that the contentment, wellbeing and lasting happiness they feel will be due to things other than the money or material possessions.

If you still believe that financial riches will provide you with happiness because it provides you with material possessions and freedom, then I'm afraid you are working to a misguided happiness business plan. The natural progression of any momentary happiness gained from money is to want more or something different because the novelty wears off and you will default back to your predisposed level of happiness. Research shows that any increased happiness gained from financial win falls will typically last no more than three months.[109]

Our search for happiness in money and material possession is erroneous. The media has its part to play in emphasising our misguided link between money and happiness as it bombards us with images of the rich and famous. We see their glamorous looking lives and their expensive lifestyle and we make the connection between material positions, wealth and fame with increased levels of happiness. Companies will also spend millions marketing their products as something we need to make us happier, creating an unconscious belief that we need their product to make our lives better.

Be mindful of the fact that your exposure to the global media and prolific marketing of the rich and famous can result in you focusing on what you do not have and rather than what you do have.

Born in 1913, my Nan used to tell me stories of her own childhood during the First and Second World Wars. Times were hard but communities pulled together and she recalled very fond memories of her early years. When I was around sixteen years old and trying to decide whether to stay on at school for higher education or head into the world of employment, my Nan said: *"You see it was much easier in my day. Life was simple back then. We didn't have a television to show us what we didn't have. We didn't have hundreds of magazines showing us all the things we didn't have. There was a local factory that I wanted to work in because my mum had worked there and that would do for me. Life was simple and we were happy."* She lived happily for ninety-nine years.

Contrary to what the media portrays, you also know that many of the rich and famous become depressed, have drug and alcohol dependency problems and even become suicidal. Having a goal or a wish to be an actor, musician or great artist can increase your happiness if it is something that you enjoy doing, gives you meaning and plays to your strengths but financial gain should be seen as the by-product and not the main goal or motivation.

A friend of mine spoke of an uncharacteristic and frank talk he once had with his father. His father worked for a large European military project that afforded him a comfortable early retirement. As my friend and his father enjoyed a glass of forty year old whiskey from the cellar, sitting in their adequate house with opulent furnishings, my friend commented on how he hoped to be as successful as his father. They begin reminiscing over the times when they had very little, when his father struggled to make ends meet and how they all used to spend their holidays in cheap caravans in Wales. They spoke of how they would sometimes go fishing together in the hope to catch some mackerel for dinner. They ruminated and laughed about those days before money became no issue and when the laughter faded away the conversation paused and my friends father looked down at the shallow glass of whiskey in his hand and said: *"If you recognise all the precious moments in your life, then you will have more success than any amount of money or job could give you."*

It is worth repeating that to want material comforts for yourself and your family is a good thing but be careful not to sacrifice the real things that provide you with lasting happiness. Obtain material possessions for yourself and your loved ones but do not hold the expectation that it will bring you lasting happiness.

It is vital that you invest wisely in targeted, evidence-based areas that you know will bring you maximum profit of lasting happiness. This is the very essence of your Business Plan for Happiness.

WORK: CREATING
HAPPINESS AT WORK

"Happiness lies in the joy of achievement and the thrill of creative effort."
Franklin D. Roosevelt

MOST OF US SPEND around one thousand eight hundred hours at work each year and therefore, work provides a lot of opportunity to reap some more happiness income.

A common belief in the work place is to work longer and harder to be more productive. Pushing to your maximum capacity at work is often seen as a way to show aptitude and a means to work yourself up the career ladder.

However, with the mind-set of working employees to their maximum for as long as possible, it is common for employees to feel neglected, worn out, stressed, unhappy and be less productive. Additionally, unhappy staff are likely to leave. Staff turnover is a huge limitation and expense to a business. It costs to advertise for a position, it costs managers time to interview for the role and it then costs more time and resources to train the new recruit. For this and many other reasons, ensuring that staff members are happy at work should be high on an employer's priority list.

To get the best out of their staff studies suggest that employers should adopt a positive support-and-nurture working framework rather than a negative push-and-punish management model. The push-and-punish model drives employees to do more and work even harder under the threat of punishment (e.g. losing a bonus for example). The support-and-nurture approach provides a positive environment for staff and instigates a positive reward management style, which is far more beneficial for business production.

Ensuring staff have a supportive structure in place, take regular breaks from their work, have full lunch breaks and work appropriate hours is shown to increase productivity. In a support-and-nurture environment, staff work smarter and more efficiently rather than harder and less effectively. Creating a positive working environment and taking time to ensure staff are happy will broaden creativity, decrease time off through sickness and build team cohesion. This results in staff who are loyal, dedicated, skilled, creative and productive [121, 122, 67]

An all too common example many companies will operate under is the target driven bonus system. This type of negatively driven system sets a single target for staff to reach and if they do not reach this target, they are punished financially by not receiving a bonus. This motivation method will suit some people, particularly those with a combination of Proactive, Towards and Thinking LAB profile (See WORK: THE LAB PROFILE), but many employers apply a bonus driven environment to *all* employees believing it delivers the best results.

The problem with a target driven structure is that some employees will reach their target and receive their bonus whilst other employees will not. Those that reach their target are given (or punished with, depending on how you view it) an even larger target to hit the following month until eventually they fail to hit target too.

In addition, this system does not take into account the level of effort required or put in by staff. The fact might be the non-bonus earners worked harder than the person who received a bonus and yet they receive no reward and, in fact, are financially punished for their hard work. This negative system can increase staff division, reducing a sense of team cohesion and research also shows that the push-and-punish system is one of the quickest ways to undermine staff motivation.[69]

STEPS TO INCREASE HAPPINESS INCOME AT WORK

There are three simple rules by which an employee can be given the opportunity to increase happiness income at work:

1: The work should be varied in order for the employee to utilise a variety of skills and talents.

2: Rather than doing small bits of projects or work, an employee should be able to work on a project from start to finish.

3: The employee must feel like their work will benefit others.

You may be an employee and therefore feel like there is little you can do to influence how you are managed. There are, however, ways to squeeze out much more commercial happiness income from your line of work. Even if you dislike your job you can find a few small ways to cash in a few pennies of happiness here and there throughout your working day. Over your one hundred and sixty hour working month those pennies of happiness will all add up in your happiness bank. You will be surprised how much you can add to your happiness bank through working life. A good place to start is to identify meaning and purpose.

WORK: THE IMPORTANCE OF
MEANING AND PURPOSE

*"How can I be useful, of what service can I be? There
is something inside me, what can it be?"*

Vincent Van Gogh

AFTER TWO YEARS WORKING for the NHS, helping to set up and
facilitate sustainable community projects to resolve local health issues,
I was offered the position of Public Health Manager. This promotion
offered a significant pay rise and career opportunities and yet I turned
down the opportunity. After careful consideration, I realised that
although it would hold the same purpose of helping others improve their
environment, health and lives (which was of value to me), the new role
would take me out of the community and replace doing what I enjoyed
with back-to-back strategy meetings which held less meaning to me.

The Public Health Managers role would not have played to my
strengths, which was to work within the community, overseeing and co-
ordinating local health services to set up and facilitate projects. Sitting in
meetings everyday would not have played to my true strengths or utilise
my skills effectively and would not have provided me with meaning.
If I had taken the promotion it would have been a poor investment in
my own Business Plan for Happiness. It would not have provided me
with meaning, which was very likely to make me unproductive and my
purpose would have reduced along with my level of happiness.

Your own work must have meaning and purpose in order for you to
bring in the ultimate income of happiness and enable you to be successful.
If your work does not provide you with meaning or purpose, you should
identify your strengths and find ways to implement them within your
work so that meaning and purpose is significantly increased.

Of course this may not be easy to do at first and if your current work does not play to your strengths or give you meaning or purpose then your mission statement is to identify what will.

MEANING:

For an activity to have meaning it needs to be in line with your values because values drive motivation and desire.

Values are created from the beliefs you hold about what is right and wrong, what is important and less important. Therefore, what you value is what you believe, and this gives you meaning and motivation in life. Some of your values will take higher priority than others. You may value justice and democracy but value peace and human life more. Therefore you could not support violence even if it was in the name of justice or democracy. Similarly, there will be many values that you have in the context of work but some will take priority and hold more meaning than others.

IDENTIFYING YOUR WORK VALUES

To identify your values and to help put them in order of priority, you need to list your work related values. Answer the following questions and follow the subsequent actions:

1. In terms of work and career, list all the things that are important to you. This list should not be what you have now in your current job, but what is important to you in any job or your ideal job. Don't list what you think you should value or what you think should be important to you; instead write down what actually is important to you. For example, I've worked with some people who miss money off of their work value list. This means one of three things: It either explains why they are broke because they don't value money or it means they are already very wealthy and work to satisfy other values rather than cash, or it will mean they aren't being truthful about what is important to them. So, in the context of work, what is important to you? Make a list.

2. You now have a list of things that are important to you in the context of work. These are some of your work values. Now ask yourself the following question: If your working role had none of your listed values, what would have to happen in order for you to stay in that job?

3. Lastly, this question should eke out a few more of your work values. Look at your list and ask, if your job contained all the values listed, what would have to happen in order for you to leave? List your answers. These are also your values so add them to your list.

4. Now you have an extensive list of what you value in the context of work or career. Now let's tidy it up. Some of your values on your list will mean the same thing to you. For example, you may have 'feeling appreciated' and 'knowing I'm doing a good job.' Do these mean the same thing to you? They may mean two separate things so leave them if they do. You may have written down "a good salary" and "financial security." Again, ask yourself what you actually mean, are they separate or do they mean the same? For those values that 'duplicate' in meaning, keep the one that encompasses all the rest and delete the others.

5. Now put them in order of priority by choosing your top ten values. This will be hard because they are all important to you, but what are the most important ones? If you read a job description that stated ten of your values, which ten would make you go for that job most?

6. Now you have your top ten values in order of importance and priority. Look at your current job and see which of your top ten values are present in your work and which ones are missing. For those that are present in your current working role, ask yourself if you can find ways to adjust or adapt your working activities to support your values more. For those values that aren't present or barely present within your current job, take time to look at all your working activities and use your creativity, your intelligence and your experience to find ways to create these values.

7. If your current career holds none of your values, my advice would be to find a job that does.

When you have identified your work related values you can identify ways to make sure your current working role supports these values and provide you with meaning. If you have meaning, you have purpose. With meaning and purpose, your lasting happiness will increase.

Purpose:

Having meaning and purpose is a happy combination but why is purpose so important to your level of work satisfaction? What is it that gives your work purpose and why? Purpose can be defined in three contexts:

1. The object toward which one strives or for which something exists; an aim or a goal.
2. A result or effect that is intended or desired; an intention.
3. Determination; resolution.

All three definitions are relevant to your work.

1: Purpose: The object toward which one strives or for which something exists; an aim or a goal

Linked closely to your values and meaning, this definition of purpose should be found from asking what it is you want to achieve in your work. Are you driven to earn more money? Are you working to climb up the career ladder? Or have you not asked this question yet?

If the latter is true then your job will be lacking in purpose. Without purpose you have nothing to strive towards, your existence at work has no goals to measure your achievements by. Having no clear purpose at work is like having no postcode to enter into your satellite navigation system. Without a postcode, your Sat. Nav. will not know why you are travelling or where to take you and you will drift nowhere.

Make a list of what you want to gain from your work. Is it to retire at sixty with a good pension? Is it to drive a bigger car or enable you to travel more? Do you want to be able to help more people? Do you simply want to provide for your family and put your children through private school or university? Perhaps you want to learn more and increase your knowledge, or perhaps you want all of these things.

Be specific with what you want. For example: *"I want to earn £3000 per month after TAX by the time I'm 40 years old"* or *"I want to have my mortgage paid off 10 years early so I can retire earlier and travel more"* or *"I want to send all my kids to college so that they can have a good start in life"* or *"I want to be a Director by the time I'm 45 years old"* or *"I want to have a 10% deposit for a house in four years time."*

Once you know what you want from work ask if your current job can provide you with this purpose. If it does not then it is time to make a plan and seek ways to give your job more purpose.

2: PURPOSE: A RESULT OR EFFECT THAT IS INTENDED OR DESIRED; AN INTENTION.

With a defined purpose you will know what you need to put in to your work and what you need to receive in return in order to achieve that purpose. Because you know what you will get from your work you also know what results you can expect. Now you have purpose, intention *and* desire.

3: PURPOSE: DETERMINATION; RESOLUTION

Whether you are working to buy a bigger house, provide more for your family, go on holiday more, travel the world more, buy your dream car, retire early, gain respect or help more people, once you know why you are working you will have purpose.

Once you have discovered what gives your work meaning and purpose, your working role will increase your desire and intention as well as develop a sense of determination to achieve your goals. With this combination, you will be focused on getting what *you* want from work rather than what work wants from you and this will increase your happiness income.

WORK: STRENGTHEN YOUR STRENGTHS

"Do what you do best. It's the purpose for which you were made."
Unknown

WHEN ASKED, ONLY ONE in every three people can suggest any of their strengths. Of those that do, strengths are listed as something they are good at. Being good at something is not necessarily a strength but perhaps merely something you have learned to do well.

Alex Linley suggests that our strengths are often mixed up with our learned behaviours.[83] The key difference between a learned behaviour and a true strength is energy. A strength is not only something you are good at but also something that energises you and something you can perform for long periods without becoming drained. You can become lost in an activity that plays to your strengths and immersed into the moment. A learned behaviour, however, is something that you enjoy for a while but instead of increasing energy levels it becomes tiring.

Traditionally, employers will not consider an employee's true strengths when hiring or developing staff. If the employee struggles in a certain area of work because it does not play to their strengths, the employer tends to send the staff member onto a training course in an attempt to strengthen their weaknesses. Research strongly suggests that it is better for businesses if individuals are hired based on strengths that match the role requirements, rather than judged on the learned behaviours shown on their c.v. In this way the employee is not only going to be effective at their job but also enjoy and be energised by their work.

Research shows that people who utilise their strengths during home and working life are:

1. Happier.[99, 91]
2. More confident.[66, 101]
3. Have higher levels of self-esteem.[66, 91]
4. Have higher levels of energy and vitality.[66]
5. Experience lower levels of stress.[121]
6. More resilient and able to cope.[25]
7. More likely to achieve their goals.[84]
8. Perform better at work.[116]
9. More engaged and committed to their work.[67, 91]

Identifying and using your strengths is extremely productive for business and therefore should be a focus for all employers, as well as an area of focus for your own Business Plan for Happiness.

Identify and utilise your strengths whilst moderating your learned behaviours and minimise tasks that involve areas of weakness whether at home, work or at play.

IDENTIFYING AND USING STRENGTHS RATHER THAN LEARNED BEHAVIOURS

To identify your own strengths Alex Linley provides ten tips to help differentiate between learned behaviours and strengths:

1. Strengths will tend to be those things that you have always been good at and enjoyed since childhood.
2. Strengths are those activities that provide you with energy.
3. Activities that play to your strengths are likely to make you feel as if it is who you really are and what you are supposed to be doing rather than fitting into a role or attempting to adapt yourself to perform.
4. Activities that play to your strengths should feel relatively effortless.
5. Pay attention to those tasks or jobs that you seek out because you enjoy them, as these activities may well be utilising your strengths.
6. Tasks that you seem to pick up and learn naturally could be using your strengths.
7. Activities that you are motivated to do are likely to be because they encompass your strengths.
8. When discussing work or home activities, notice your tone of voice. Those that use your strengths will be reflected in the energy and passion within your voice.
9. Equally, some of the words used when talking about activities that involve your strengths will be reflected. E.g: *"I love to..."* or *"It's great when..."*
10. On a list of things to do, the ones that tend to get done over and above all other tasks are likely to involve the use of your strengths.

For a more in depth assessment of your strengths visit: www.strengths2020.com

WORK: THE LAB PROFILE

"Do not judge your friend until you stand in his place"
Unknown

Identifying and utilising your strengths is such a major component within your Business Plan for Happiness because it will improve the happiness income received across all aspects of your life.

Here is an introduction to another way to identify and incorporate your strengths.

Positive Psychology is a new branch of psychological study that investigates well-being and optimal functioning but before its official title, there were researchers who had already contributed a great deal in this field.

During the 1970's a psychology student called Richard Bandler at University of California, Santa Cruz, joined in study with John Grinder to investigate what made people successful in business? What were the processes that made people outstanding at their skills? And could other people learn to replicate these processes for behaviour change? Rather than being interested in *why* these individuals were exceptional at what they did, Bandler and Grinder studied *how* they did what they did. The theory followed that if they could learn *how*, then they could replicate that person's success. This was the beginning of: Neuro-linguistic-programming (NLP).

Bandler and Grinder's findings conformed to Noam Chomsky's thesis (Professor of Linguistics & Philosophy at MIT) around transformational grammar, which suggested that individuals delete, distort and generalise information to form an outlook of the world. [30, 31]

Chomsky's delete, distort and generalise filter system explains why different people can report different experiences of the same situation.

It provides an explanation into the causes of miscommunication, misinterpretation and explains how some people have strengths in certain activities whilst others struggle. It can even predict how we respond and behave in certain situations.

Similar to a computer system, our filters act as neurological programmes within our brain. These programmes have been termed Meta-Programs.

Following on from the work of Chomsky, Bandler and Grinder, Roger Bailey developed the Language and Behaviour Profile (LAB). Bailey postulated that if it were possible to identify an individual's Meta-Program (i.e. what information they pay attention to and are therefore motivated by) it would enable us to communicate far more effectively and influence motivation more effectively.

The LAB profile helps explain why you have strengths in certain activities and weaknesses in others. Your weaknesses are not flaws but caused by the fact that you filter out some information and therefore do not process that information as effectively or accurately. Your strengths come to life in activities containing information that is not filtered out, causing a stream of information that you find stimulating.

The LAB profile can provide you with a more in-depth understanding of your strengths and accurately identify how you can play to these strengths whilst also getting the most out of other people.

It is important to understand that Meta-Programs are context specific. That is to say an individual can display different levels of Meta-Programs in different situations. The situation we are interested in here is within the context of work and the working environment.

Meta-Program: Proactive & Reactive

Proactive individuals are those who dive into a situation with little or no need to be managed. In the extreme case, a highly proactive individual will leap straight into a project without much preparation or guidance. Proactive individuals are very good at getting the job done and managers can point them in the right direction and then let them get on with the job. Highly proactive individuals will need minimal management but can lose sight of the end goal because they are moving full-steam ahead, therefore, it is important to ensure they remain on target. Proactive individuals will steamroll anyone in their path and can be an asset in an aggressive sales environment.

Reactive individuals tend to wait to be told what to do and once the task is complete they will need to be told what the next job is. Reactive individuals will take their time to analyse the situation and act with caution. Extreme Reactive people will need consistent feedback and task managing. Reactive individuals are suited to analytical roles or customer services.

Sixty to sixty-five percent of people will have a balance of Proactive and Reactive profiles in their employed role so it can be easy to identify yourself and others who fall on the high end of this Meta-Program.

META-PROGRAM: TOWARDS & AWAY FROM

Some individuals will be motivated towards a target to gain or achieve a goal, whilst others will be motivated to avoid or move away from a situation.

Towards people will be driven to achieve a particular goal and work well when given targets to meet, deadlines to achieve and, at the higher end of this profile, they are unable to foresee or factor in obstacles or problems. These individuals are typically good at making and maintaining financial gains because they are focused on attaining assets.

Away From people will work to avoid problems and obstacles and are driven to move away from a situation. These individuals can find it hard to maintain financial security because they are motivated to move away from poverty but when they attain enough distance, their motivation to continue to make money will dwindle until such time that they are close enough to poverty to be motivated once again. These individuals are suited to working roles that incorporate crisis management, health & safety or project management because they will foresee the potential problems and hurdles to overcome.

Only twenty percent of the population will have a balance of both Towards and Away From profiles, leaving eighty percent having a Meta-Program that falls into either Away From or Towards.

META-PROGRAM: INTERNAL & EXTERNAL

Some people are motivated by internal feedback whilst others require external feedback.

Internal people assess their productivity and work based on how it feels to them. They will have their own internal checklist of how they are performing. Telling a highly Internal staff member that they are doing a good job will do little to motivate them because they will already know. Internal people will make their own decisions on how they are progressing. They are good at self-monitoring, they are self-motivated and therefore suited to independent roles.

External people require external feedback on how they are progressing. To motivate External staff, managers will need to provide consistent and regular positive feedback to let them know that they are working well. External individuals work well as part of a team so that they can consistently gain feedback from others and adjust their work accordingly.

Forty percent of us will be either Internally or Externally driven.

META-PROGRAM: OPTIONS & PROCEDURES

Some individuals love to work to a structure and a set of procedures whilst others work to their own creative interpretation of what is needed to get the job done.

Options people will be motivated by possibilities and driven by creating new ways of doing things. Their strength is to think creatively, produce ideas and work well as part of a think tank. However, because the creative aspect of project options and possibilities energises them, their motivation tends to waiver beyond the creative stage and they can have difficulty finishing a task. Options people can seem hard to manage because their strengths do not lie with following set protocol and they will be restricted and unproductive if not given several options to achieve the task at hand.

Procedures staff have strengths in working to a set structure and suited to strategy planning or roles that involve rules and a 'right' way of doing things (such as in Human Resources for example). A person with a combination of Procedures and Towards profiles will also do very well in sales. Procedures people can be a manager's dream especially if they also have an External Meta-Program profile because they will not only toe the line but listen and act upon managerial feedback as well.

In the context of work forty percent of us are on the Options or Procedures end of this Meta-Program continuum.

META-PROGRAM: SPECIFIC & GENERAL

Rather than being what motivates an individual, the remaining Meta-Programs reflect how an individual processes information to work at their best.

Specific individuals love to work with detail. On the high end of this profile, these individuals want as much information on a subject as possible. They often give themselves away by giving lots of descriptive and in-depth detail during a conversation. Specific individuals work well in accounts, computer programming or roles that involve lots of data. Individuals with a Specific profile will also be suited to management of complex projects as they will thrive on assessing all the aspects of the detail, but can significantly delay the start of a project because of the fact.

General individuals do not thrive in the detail of project facilitation but they do have a good ability to conceptualise a project in the first place. Staff with a highly General Meta-Program are able to see several steps ahead and visualise the overall outcome or direction of a project. They find detail dull and unsatisfying and their conversations will tend to be concise and to the point. Individuals that fall under the high end of the General spectrum will typically do well in positions of management as they will provide the vision of how to get to a business goal and then rely on their team (ideally consisting mostly of Specific individuals) to work out the detail of how to make it happen.

In the context of work, only around fifteen percent of us have a high Specific profile but sixty percent of us have high General profiles. The remainder will fall somewhere in between.

META-PROGRAM: FEELING, CHOICE & THINKING

Particularly useful in understanding how people react to stress is the Meta-Program of Feeling, Choice and Thinking.

Feeling profile refers to individuals who are not productive in jobs that involve a high level of stress. These individuals are sensitive and their emotions are triggered easily. This makes them ideal for creative roles where their emotions can be expressed through their work and they are free to open up to their emotions.

Choice profile people tend to monitor their emotions after they are triggered. That is to say; whilst Feeling profilers will experience an emotion and stay within it, Choice profilers will initially experience the emotion before making a choice to move on from it. These individuals have strengths in people managing because they can empathise with other staff when needed but turn the emotions off again when out of the situation or when they decide it is no longer appropriate.

Thinking people show little emotion and assess things analytically. They work well in highly stressed working environments because they can switch off from the emotional side of things and rationalise the job at hand. They work well on their own rather than within a team due to their practical way of thinking and do not easily empathise with the emotions of others.

Seventy percent of us will have a Choice profile, leaving the remaining thirty percent of the population divided between Feeling and Thinking profiles.

These are a few of the Meta-Programs that will help identify your strengths, what motivates you at work and what roles will also give you energy. This enables you to perform well and bring in happiness income at work. Meta-Programs help explain why these are your strengths due to the delete, distort and generalise filter system that makes you pay attention to different information.

Spend time working out how to maximise your strengths at work and delegate or reduce as many tasks that do not use them. In some cases this may not be possible but even small adjustments can help tip your working life towards your strengths and increase your income of happiness.

The following table will help you identify your own LAB profile. By answering each question, it will give you an idea of your own internal filters. For more detail information visit: ***www.labprofile.net***

Category	Question	Types
EXTERNAL BEHAVIOUR	"When it's time to recharge your batteries do you like to be alone or with someone else?"	– Introvert = Recharges best when on their own – Extrovert = Recharges best in social situations
INTERNAL PROCESS	"In gathering information about something new that you are learning do you prefer the facts or are you more interested in the relationship between the facts"	– Sensor – details = Prefers working with clear facts and enjoys the details of information – Intuitor – big picture = Prefers working with larger concepts, strategies and ideas
INTERNAL STATE	"Is it more important for you that you are thought of as a reasonable and rational person or a caring and feeling person?"	– Thinking = evaluates external world based on what they think about it. They are logical – Feeling – More into values and feelings
TIME	"If you are going to go somewhere to do something do you want to plan it or do you want to just take it as it comes?"	– Judger = Works best with lists, enjoys planning, and is organised – Perceiver = Tends to take things as they come
DIRECTION FILTER	"What do you want in a car, relationship or job?" "What's important to you about a car, relationship or job?"	– Toward = Will state results and performance – Both towards and away equal – Away From = Will state what they don't want

REASON FILTER

"Why are you choosing to do what you are doing?"

- Possibility = Will state possible outcomes
- Necessity = Will state the things they need from the outcome
- Both = Will state both possibilities and needs

FRAME OF REFERENCE FILTER

"How do you know when you're doing a good job?"

- Internal = Will cite the facts they know
- External = Will rely on feedback
- Balance of both
- Internal with external check = Will state the facts they know but need to check via feedback
- External with internal check = Will agree with feedback if it is in line with what they think

CONVINCER DEMONSTRATION FILTER

"How do you know when someone else is good at what they do?"

- See = They see results
- Hear = They hear results
- Read = They read results
- Do = They assess on what they do

CONVINCER DEMONSTRATION FILTER "How often does someone have to demonstrate competence to you before you're convinced?"	– Automatic = Make decision straight away – Number of times = Need to assess several times – Period of time = Need to go away and assess – Consistent = Need consistent assessment
MANAGEMENT DIRECTION FILTER "Do you know what you need to do to be a success on a job?" "Do you know what someone else needs to do to do a good job?" "Do you find it easy or not easy to tell him/her?"	– Self and others = Has an idea but needs guidance – Self only = Knows themselves – Others only = Needs guidance
ACTION FILTER "When you come into a situation do you usually act quickly after sizing it up, or do you do a complete study of all the consequences and then act?"	– Active = Acts quickly – Reflective = Needs evidence – Both = Equal amounts of action with evidence – Inactive = Finds it hard to take action either way
AFFILIATION FILTER "Tell me about a work situation in which you were the happiest, a one-time event"	– Independent player = Likes to work on their own initiative – Team player = Likes to work as part of a team – Manager player = Likes to manage others

WORK PREFERENCE FILTER "Tell me about a work situation in which you were the happiest, a one-time event"	– Things = Cites the things they were doing – Systems = Cites the structure and organisational processes – People = Cites the people and social network
PRIMARY INTEREST FILTER "What's your favourite restaurant? Tell me about it"	– People = Cites the people that attend – Place = Cites the type of venue – Things = Cites the things at the venue – Activity = Cites the activities at the venue – Information = Cites the details of information at the venue
CHUCK SIZE FILTER "If we were going to do a project together, would you want to know the big picture first, or the details first? Would you really need to know the…(ask the opposite reply)	– Specific = Will give detailed information – Global = Will give an overview

EMOTIONAL STRESS RESPONSE	
"Tell me about a situation (context related) that gave you trouble, a one-time event"	– Thinking = May find it hard to state a stressful time or state practical problems – Feeling = May state emotions involved in a situation that involve other people – Choice = May state too much workload or relate to decision making

TIME STORAGE FILTER	
"What direction is the past and what direction is your future for you?"	– Through time = Will indicate a direction that doesn't pass through their body – In time = Will indicate a direction that passes through their body

LISTENING STYLE	
"If someone you knew quite well said to you, "I'm thirsty", would you: – Find it interesting, but probably do nothing about it or… – Would you feel really compelled to do something about it?"	– Literal = Takes comments literally and finds it hard to read into a comment – Inferential = Reads into comments and understand hints

WORK: SPREADING HAPPINESS

"Happiness quite unshared can scarcely be called happiness; it has no taste."
Charlotte Brontë

SOMETIMES IT CAN BE hard to view the human race as being inherently compassionate but without other peoples kindness you would have nothing.

It is due to the intentional and unintentional kindness of others that you were born, born safely, fed, clothed, nurtured, sheltered, got jobs, got paid, had holidays and felt the love of friends and family. Without the help from other people you would not be here. Without giving and receiving with compassionate minds the ripple of happiness will not spread.

In 1995 I worked at a summer camp for underprivileged children in Pennsylvania, USA. Many of the children were either, directly or indirectly, affiliated with gangs and many had experienced great sadness and tragedy. With this type of upbringing, it was unsurprising to discover that the children had an inability to share. Whether it was with their food or friendships, the children were brought up in a dog-eat-dog environment. Even the very young children (8 years old) seemed to hold the belief that in order to get somewhere in life and attain the things they wanted, it was a matter of holding on tightly to whatever they had whilst looking for a method to take what others have got. This isolated view made it hard for them to trust each other or accept a helping hand from staff and it took a long time for them to form new social networks. Incidences of theft were common, which created a self-fulfilling prophecy and mistrust became even more prevalent.

To help the children recognise the benefits of sharing, trusting and gratitude, I set up a practical 'game'.

Myself and a few other staff gathered groups of children into the Tabernacle. We gave each child one, two or three small gifts as they entered. After quietening some protests from the kids who had less than others I began to tell a true story about the wise man who gave to other people.

The story tells the tale of a wise man who lived in a small hut on the outskirts of a village. The wise man's hut consisted of one room containing a small bed, a simple cooking area and a wash area in the corner. Even though he possessed very little the wise man could always be found helping his friends and villagers whenever and with whatever he could. Some people in the village would take advantage of his kindness and take from him without giving anything back but the wise man kept on giving. Over the years, everyone knew the wise man because he had helped everyone in the village at some point.

One day a great flood washed through the village and swept away the wise man's hut and everything he owned was gone. After the floodwater had subsided, the news of the wise man's situation spread through the village. Soon the entire village was walking up the hill to where the wise man's hut used to be and there they found the wise man sitting on a rock. The villagers started to help him. The tailor he had once helped carry cloth made him clothes. The baker he had helped gather wood for the oven gave him bread. The farmer he had once helped with the harvest gave him corn, eggs and a goat for milk. The carpenters and the woodmen gathered together everyone else the wise man had helped over the years to build him a new, bigger and more comfortable home. In just a short time, through the kindness and gratitude of other people the wise man had everything he could ever wish for and was never without friends.

After telling this story I asked the children to stand up and walk amongst each other. I then, periodically stopped them and told them to give away the gifts they were given, to the nearest persons to them. Reluctantly the children began giving their gifts away to each other and to their surprise, no sooner had they given something away to one child they were given something in return by another child. At points they would have one gift and at other points they would have several. Moans and protests soon turned into laughter and friendly chatter between the children as they recognised that giving to others did not reduce their possessions and it felt good too.

Research supports the feelings of well-being those children experienced and the return in happiness they received. Michael Norton (Harvard Business School) conducted an experiment whereby he gave two groups of people the same amount of money to spend. Group A was told to spend the money on themself whilst Group B was asked to spend the money on someone else. Norton found that by spending the money on other people Group B not only increased their levels of happiness to a greater degree than Group A but their level of happiness remained higher for a significantly longer period of time after the event. Group A experienced an initial level of happiness gained from their new possessions but dropped back to their original level of happiness shortly after the novelty had worn off.[48]

Gratitude provides a good level of happiness income depending on whom you give to. Receiving gifts of unsolicited kindness from close family members seems to bring little happiness effect because it is anticipated or expected. Equally, receiving gifts of kindness from someone who is perceived to easily afford the gift does little to increase levels of gratitude. However, receiving a gift of kindness from someone you do not know provides a large income of happiness.[87] The receiver experiences increased levels of happiness from the kindness of strangers and there is also a significant kickback for the giver too. The person giving feels happier and the person who received the kindness feels happier. Gratitude spreads happiness.

Furthermore, research shows that if you receive a gift of kindness from a stranger you are much more likely to do the same for someone else.[4, 87] Additional research carried out by Fowler and Christakis[55] suggests that happiness spreads like a smile. Fowler and Christakis' research shows that simply socialising with happy and kind people will increase your level of well-being. Their study shows that people who interact with happy people on a daily basis, whether directly or as part of a social group, are likely to become happier themselves.

RANDOM ACTS OF KINDNESS

About once a week (or more) perform random acts of kindness for people you know, or better still, for people you don't know. Examples could be:

− Buy a lottery ticket and give it to someone you don't know. They may think it's strange but hey, they'll take it and you can walk away with a smile knowing that the happiness is very likely to spread.

− Do something for a neighbour. Knock on their door with some cakes you've baked, some fruit you've picked from your garden or wash their car for them or mow their lawn.

− Send someone some flowers or leave some at a grave of someone you've never known.

− Help out at a soup kitchen at Christmas for a few hours.

− Leave a greeting card on the train or bus marked "For the person who finds this" (Don't leave packages obviously). Inside the card write something like; "Hoping you have a pleasant day and that your life is filled with love and laughter"

The list could go on.

The list of possibilities for your random acts of kindness is endless although there is a word of warning. Every act of kindness must always be accompanied with wisdom. You must think about the consequences of your kindness. Giving money to a homeless person may enable them to buy drugs or alcohol - not all homeless people are on drugs or alcoholics but it must be considered. Giving someone a self-help book may be interpreted wrongly. Express Emotional Intelligence and consider the person that will recieve your kindness and assess with wisdom how they may view it. Good intentions can have negative impact so give random kindness with wise abundance.

PLAY: PAY ATTENTION

"I, not events, have the power to make me happy or unhappy today. I can choose which it shall be. Yesterday is dead, tomorrow hasn't arrived yet. I have just one day, today, and I'm going to be happy in it."
Groucho Marx

OTHER THAN HAVING A vague idea about Einstein's theory of relativity, we do not spend much time thinking about the concept of time. We have an underlying concept of time passing from the future, through the present moment and into the past. It is not something we tend to consciously see in this way but we have an idea of what has to be done tomorrow. We may be thinking about washing the car, seeing friends, going to Spanish class, playing a sport or going on a date or getting work done. These activities are scheduled into our future and when that moment arrives the activity 'moves' into the past as an event that has happened, something that has been and gone. This is how we tend to consciously or unconsciously view time.

With our busy work schedules and diaries full of meetings, family commitments and chores, we always have things scheduled for the following day, week or month and we end up living in the future and not appreciating, savouring or taking time to absorb the moment. Even whilst we are taking part in the activity we have been looking forward to, we can find ourselves thinking about what we have to do afterwards rather then savouring the moment.

A holiday is a typical example: From the moment you book the holiday you begin to look forward and count down the months, weeks and days in anticipation. You begin to wish time would speed up so you can get on the plane and enjoy your holiday. Then the holiday arrives and you are sitting on the plane wishing the journey away and wanting to be at your destination. The plane lands and you are up and out of your seat grabbing hand luggage before the seat belt sign is switched off because you are desperate to get to the resort. Arriving at the resort you now urgently want to get a drink by the pool because then your holiday can begin. Now you are by the pool with a drink in your hand wondering where to eat that night and what sights you should see tomorrow. You begin to make mental plans around the logistics of your sightseeing and how you should schedule things in for the week so you don't miss any of it (The irony!). You continue the rest of your holiday living in the future, wanting for the next thing and before you know it you are wondering where the time has gone as your holiday draws to an end and you wish there was more time.

This is how most of us live our entire lives. We wish time away to get to an event in the future but when the event arrives we are already thinking about somewhere or something else rather than soaking up the experience. We never really experience our lives because we are constantly wishing each moment away and mentally living somewhere else in the future.

Because of your busy time orientated schedules, it can be common for your mind to view life like a conveyor belt of time that delivers experiences from the future before it is carried away into your past. In reality your mind has got it wrong. There is no such thing as time per se; there is only the present moment. Where does an experience really come from? A moment that brings a different experience into your life does not *come* from the future, as if it were something waiting to happen on the conveyer belt. The date you fly out on your next holiday is not ticking towards you like the hands of a clock. Life takes place in the present moment, which is a constant, seamless continuation taking place right in front of your eyes.

The past is just a collection of memories and therefore no longer exists and the future is a collection of things that are yet to exist. Therefore, neither the past nor the future exist. The future is only a concept in your mind, a concept of time that is yet to take place. It is nothing but a potential experience that may or may not happen. The only true constant existence is the present moment that is happening right HERE and right NOW.

Being truly immersed in the present moment is a blissful experience as all the future scheduling disappears leaving you with life as it happens in the moment. The mind-created-self is born from thought and therefore, it will always live in the past or future. Very similar to the experience of deep meditation, savouring the moment leaves no place for your mind-created-self because it cannot survive in the present moment.

Your mind-created-self runs towards the future with the anticipation of receiving something that will make you happy, but say you managed to reach all your wants and needs, would you then be happy? Perhaps for a short while but your mind-created-self lives in the past and future and because neither exist, it will always have questions, anticipation, wants and needs that can never be fulfilled. The mind-created-self can never be truly satisfied because it seeks happiness tomorrow, which will never come around.

As Dr Tal Ben-Shahar [12] points out, in the West we spend all our time and effort chasing goals and then mistaking the relief of achieving our goal for happiness before setting off once again with eyes set on something new. The relief we feel once arriving at our destination reinforces and conditions the belief that achieving a goal is what makes us happy rather than the journey towards the achievement. The journey becomes seen as a burden and something inconvenient that has to be endured to get to our 'happiness. This creates even more feelings of relief once we reach our destination and creates the misinterpretation that relief is happiness.

When I was about twelve years old my dad and I were going on a hike. I remember my father telling me that at the end of the journey I would see the most amazing thing I was ever likely to see. My father told me how this 'thing' was a secret kept within our family and passed on from father to son and now it was my turn.

Excitedly I filled my bag with my survival kit consisting of a blunt table knife with a piece of copper piping for a handle, my candles, water proof matches and a change of clothes. The night before the hike my mind was full and racing with what I would see on the adventure.

As soon as I woke early the next morning, my eyes sprung open and my mind raced off once again. I jumped out of bed, quickly dressed put on my walking shoes and grabbed my survival backpack. Gobbling up my breakfast we set off in the car. After about an hour we parked at the foot of some woods and I leapt out of the car and immediately started quizzing my father about the secret but he just said: *"you'll see".*

We walked into the woods and continued up the hill, traversing rivers and working together to navigate the wilderness. Along the journey, we stopped periodically for my father to teach me how to read the map, we helped each other across harder terrain and I remember laughing as my dad slipped in the mud. I also saw a wild deer for the first time. We stumbled across it whilst it was grazing and for a moment, that seemed like a lifetime, the deer and I were frozen in a gaze before it turned, hopped twice, and disappeared into the forest. I remember being able to hear the pebbles rolling on the bottom of a fast moving stream. I remember my father pointing out the nature that was hiding all around us. I remember lots about that hike.

After a couple of hours we emerged through the thicket to a clearing at the top of the hill. There was a stunning view across the valley, which we admired for several moments in silence. The mist made the lowland look like water and the sun periodically touched my face as it darted in and out of the fast moving cloud. My trance was eventually broken as my mind brought me swiftly back to the reality of our mission: to see "the most amazing thing I was ever likely to see". I was instantly filled with eagerness which my father saw as I looked up at him. He smiled and I watched him walk off, searching the ground beneath his feet before picking something up. Rushing over I looked into his hand to see "most amazing thing I was ever likely to see". It was a small unremarkable stone. Not saying a single word my father placed the stone in my hand and I examined it for its special qualities. I think I mentioned a few interesting colours and contours but mostly I remember being disappointed but my father told me to keep it safe so I put the stone in my pocket and we headed back home.

I still have the stone and can recall each moment spent on that adventure.

> *"It is good to have an end to journey towards, but*
> *it is the journey that matters in the end."*
> *Ursula Le Guin. The Left Hand of Darkness*

Professor of psychology at the University of California, Sonja

Lyubomirsky was given a five-year grant from the National Institute of Mental Health to conduct research into the possibility of permanently increasing levels of happiness. Her findings suggests that spending time living in the present moment is one of the fundamental elements to permanently increase happiness and therefore, should be a major part of your own Business Plan for Happiness.

There are two methods to promote living in the present moment:

1. Creating a state of Flow
2. Savouring

CREATING A STATE OF FLOW

Flow is a state of complete optimum experience causing harmony within any action.[37]

Flow can be likened to being *'in the zone'*. Being *'in the zone'* is how you would describe the experience of being completely absorbed within a task or activity to the point where you can become unaware of your surroundings with no concept of time or of yourself. It feels as if you are one with the task or as if you literally lose yourself within the activity. This is the state of Flow.

In deep Flow, there is little or no self-awareness and therefore, no cares about other people's views. A person in Flow loses their mind-created-self and is free to enjoy their activity with no consciousness of what is happening around them. Flow can therefore be a true state of bliss and sense of transcendence. Flow can be achieved in any activity such as dancing, painting, writing, presenting, coaching and teaching, or in fact, any strength based activity within home, rest, work or play.

The key to making any goal or task into one that will boost daily happiness is to achieve a state of Flow. Flow helps you grow and achieve your goals with real satisfaction and deep enjoyment. Achieving a state of Flow is often a natural phenomenon in those that perform tasks and activities that utilise their strengths fully. To purposefully create states of Flow you need the following:

a) Set yourself a goal to achieve. What have you always wanted to achieve? You need to be able to measure your progress to enable you to know that you are achieving this goal. Each step or measurement is one step closer.

With accurate assessment of your progress and with constant feedback, you can easily make adjustments and changes to behaviour and strategy to stay on target. Without this, you will get bored and have no clear purpose for motivation.

The challenges you set your self should be matched with your existing skills and you can develop skill over time. However, when challenges are too far from your current skill level, a state of Flow cannot be achieved and the task is unlikely to be enjoyable. So, if you are attempting to achieve something completely new, see what else you can do that matches your skills to begin with and work up from there.

b) With a step-by-step plan to attain your goals and with consistent feedback of your progress you will experience focus and directed attention. Whether your chosen activity is to run a half marathon or practise the techniques within this Business Plan for Happiness, if you approach it in a structured and measurable manner you will attain your goals and create a state of Flow whilst doing it.

In Flow you will have a single direction of thought and focus. You will gain inner harmony, feelings of achievement, a driven sense of purpose and immersion in the task. This adds up to a large amount in happiness income.

c) Within Flow your everyday tensions and frustrations are removed. The Flow activity will become your 'timeout' and create a centred feeling of living in the moment.

It is important to understand that this is very different from escapism such as watching T.V. Such mindless tasks typically involve dulling the senses of reality and moves development backwards. Attaining a state of Flow creates an enhanced state of reality that is moving and improving your development forwards.

d) The tasks that will enable you to reach your desired goal should be performed on the edge of your skill whilst remaining in control. If it is too easy there is no challenge, no achievement and no sense of purpose. Activities that are mindless or well within your capability will not take you anywhere in terms of development or experience.

Having the skills to feel in control of the activity will increase your confidence and push you towards your target. Working on the edge of your skills and capabilities will challenge the senses and Flow will occur.

e) You may have experienced Flow yourself? It is common for dancers, athletes, painters or musicians to experience a deep state of Flow. Flow takes you beyond the mind-created-self, beyond the Ego and within the moment. With practise, Flow becomes very similar to the state experienced through regular meditation.

Once out of the Flow state, Csikszentmihalyi (the leading researcher into Flow) found that confidence levels are increase along with a sense of well-being and a desire to enhance future Flow. Flow increases confidence, develops your skills and your strengths, which provides happiness through meaning and purpose.

f) Similar to the benefits of meditation, Flow causes a sense of oneness with the present moment. Flow state activities induce savouring of the moment where there is no concept of future or past, which is a very peaceful and happy place to be. To incorporate a state of Flow into your work, rest and play is a significant part of this Business Plan for Happiness.

Csikszentmihalyi clarifies between pleasure and a state of Flow. Although Flow is a pleasurable experience, it is fundamentally different to pleasure. Pleasure can be achieved by anyone without the need for skill and pleasure can be an innate predisposition but does not help us grow. Flow is enjoyable in any situation. The experience is pleasurable but fundamentally it involves skill and supports personal growth which cannot be said for all pleasures.

Flow requires attention and it is this attention that reflects your own consciousness. If your consciousness is organised and controlled with Flow you can achieve enjoyment in any situation and have fun accomplishing your goals. As Csikszentmihalyi says: ***"Ordered consciousness is effective"***

DEDICATION TO CREATING FLOW

Anyone can achieve a state of Flow but you must have the following mindset as a vow:

1. I will clarify my goals. I will clarify the feedback I need, to know that I am reaching my goals. Based on the feedback I recieve, I will know how I must adjust my own behaviour to attain my goals.

2. I will centre myself and sink into the moment to immerse myself into my goal. I will identify common distractions so I know how to avoid these distractions of mind and environment to ensure I can control my attention.

3. I always have a choice. I know there is a choice so therefore I also have control.

4. I am committed to achieving this goal. This is my choice. I choose to achieve this goal for my own sake and this is of utmost importance to my well-being and happiness. I will plan and acurately show all committment to this task, even with day-to-day trivial things. I recognise developing a state of Flow in my activities will bring me a wealth of happiness.

5. I am prepared to challenge myself. I will not settle for simple pleasures that dull my senses, I will keep striving forwards to develop better skills and achieve more.

Saying it is of course one thing, doing it is another and that's where determination and committment comes in.

SAVOURING

Savouring has been defined as any thought or behaviour capable of generating, intensifying and prolonging enjoyment.[20] By this definition, the increase in happiness through savouring can be achieved by stepping back and 'stopping to smell the roses'. The concept and benefits of savouring can also be accomplished by reminiscing on positive past experiences and visualising optimistic future outcomes.

To truly experience your life, take time out regularly to stop and savour the moments past, present and yet to come. When reaching a moment you have been looking forward to make sure you stop to enjoy it. Take time to absorb the moment and truly experience it in the present.

Once your event is over, reminisce on it (that is of course if it turned out to be as much fun as you anticipated) and think about how wonderful it will be to do something similar in the future.

Remember that it is the moments within your journey where happiness can be found. The relief you get from being de-stressed or finishing chores should not be mistaken for happiness. Relief is pleasurable but it can only be experienced after something unpleasant. Therefore, mistaking happiness for relief reinforces the belief that you must suffer to be happy. This is not true and lasting happiness is not synonymous with relief.

"The key is to keep in mind, even as one forgoes some present gain for the sake of a larger future gain, that the objective is to spend as much time as possible engaged in activities that provide both present and future benefit."
Tal Ben-Shahar

Imagine that you are an actor in a play at a theatre. You are back stage constantly thinking of the next scene, getting ready for your next part, thinking about your next line soon to take place in the future. There may be parts of the play that you enjoy and are looking forward to and parts that you are feeling apprehensive about, in either case, you are constantly preparing yourself for the next scene and once that scene is done you may briefly look back to evaluate your performance before focusing once again on your next scene.

This actor is much like the life of a Rat Racer. Whilst the Rat

Racing actor dashes about behind the curtain, the audience is completely relaxed and enjoying the show. The audience is not thinking too much about what might be coming up in the show or what just happened, the audience is simply sitting, watching and enjoying the play as it unfolds in front of their eyes. The audience is akin to the person who regularly savours the present moment, who creates a state of Flow in many activities and meditates daily.

Your life is the play itself and your mind-created-self is the actor on the stage. The actor is running around constantly living in the future and the past by reflecting on scenes gone and waiting on scenes to come. The moments between scenes are an annoyance to the actor and seen as something to be endured in order to get to the next scene. The relief felt once the play is over is then mistaken for happiness.

To have lasting happiness in life you must join the audience as often a possible, particularly when you find yourself sliding back on stage as the Rat Racing actor. Step off the stage frequently and stop worrying about what might be or what has been. Stop wishing time away to get into the future or waiting for the future to arrive because you will be wishing and waiting all your life. Savour the present moment that carries you to your goals. Take time out to truly experience these moments through all your senses.

Once you are off the stage and enjoying life as a member of the audience rather than a Rat Racing actor, you will become still within the moment and enjoy watching the excitement of your life as it unfolds.

DO WHAT YOU ENJOY DOING

Avoid remaining a Rat Racer and escape from Hedonic pleasures that only bring sporadic and momentary income of relief or pleasure, the goals you set yourself must be intrinsically motivated. That is to say the task should provide you with good feelings and bring enjoyment through simply taking part in the activity rather than being seen as a hurdle to overcome to reach an end destination.

It is important not to confuse savouring the moment with stepping out of life and society altogether. Those with no concept of time tend to be very hedonistic because they have little or no sense of consequence for their actions. Individuals who live completely in the present with no thought for the future tend to engage in unhealthy lifestyle behaviours such as drug taking.[76] They are also likely to struggle with education and find it hard holding down a job.[126]

Using the theatre analogy again, you can still be in the audience enjoying the show whilst also having an idea of where the plot is heading. In the same way, you can live in the present moment and still have a concept of where you are heading in life. Especially by creating Flow state activities, you are able to have a very precise and accurate concept of your future and each moment within your day is savoured as a complementary behaviour that is carrying you towards your goal. Research indicates that people who have a clear idea of their future goals are happier across all aspects of their life. You have a choice of what movie you go to see at the cinema and you have a choice what life you want to experience.

PLAY: BE SOCIAL

"Happiness is only real when shared."
Christopher McCandless

PEOPLE ARE MORE IMPORTANT to your own happiness than perhaps you realise.

There is nothing wrong with introverts finding quiet time to themselves and create their own space, they still enjoy social occasions as much as their extroverted friends but as an introvert, they have to make a conscious effort to see friends and family more. It is not a chore or hard work seeing them, but introverts have to be conscious of the fact that they can get wrapped up in their own introverted world at times. Unless they are conscious of this, it can be weeks at a time before speaking with their parents, inviting friends over or attend parties when invited.

I mention this because if you are an introvert you need to be aware of this and you will need to put in a little more effort to be more social because it does not come as naturally to you as it does with extroverts.

If you are an extrovert then you will typically have no trouble keeping in touch and meeting up with friends and relatives.

Being social and spending time in social settings is an extremely important part of your Business Plan for Happiness. Regardless of whether you are an introvert or extrovert, you should spend some time the with people you like because it will enhance your state of well-being.[61]

GET IN CONTACT AND BE SOCIABLE

This is a short section because the practical application is simple; get in touch with people more often and spend more time in social settings with the people you like.

Start revisiting your address book because the consensus is that you require up to seven hours in social settings each day to maintain or improve well-being (Gallup-Healthways Wellbeing Index poll).

PLAY: MOVE YOUR BAD SELF

"Lack of activity destroys the good condition of every human being, while movement and methodical physical exercise save it and preserve it."

Plato

THERE IS A FINE line between physical activity and exercise because they are interlinked and one can very easily be adapted to create the other.

Physical activity involves body movement that raises metabolic rate higher than that at rest. Exercise on the other hand, can be defined as physical activity that is planned, structured and repetitive for the purpose of increasing metabolic rate for health.

Given these definitions, exercise need not be a sweat saturated, gym grunting, body idolising affair; exercise can be the adjustment of any physical activity of your choice to become more structured and rhythmical for the purpose of making you healthier, fitter and happier.

Is exercise really that important for happiness?

If the physical and mental benefits of exercise were to be found in a pharmaceutical pill, it would be the most effective medicine ever made for extending your quality of life.

Up to a point, there is a clear inverse relationship between physical activity and ill-health. In other words, the more physically active an individual is (up to a point) the less likely they are to die prematurely from diseases such as coronary heart disease, stroke, type 2 diabetes, hypertension, kidney disease and certain cancers.[27, 44, 45, 46]

Through regular, appropriate exercise, the entire body and biological system becomes more efficient and effective. Muscles become stronger making daily activities less tiring. Blood capillary networks increase, dispersing the flow of blood into more muscle tissue and lowering blood pressure. A more prolific systemic system also makes oxygen and nutrient delivery easier, which means the heart does not have to work as hard and heart rate decreases. Exercise stimulates cell rejuvenation that helps keep your skin healthy and maintains your youthful looks. Regular exercise stimulates muscular-skeletal co-ordination helping to maintain balance, reflexes and agility. Resistance or light impact exercisers such as weight lifting and walking, significantly increase and maintain bone density, which reduces the risk of osteoporosis.[27]

Taking part in regular exercise improves all aspects of body functioning meaning you will be less tired, be able to do more, keep active in later life, prevent falls, whilst also looking and feeling younger than your sedentary friends. Exercise generally means that you can enjoy a good quality of life for much longer.

These are some of the mechanisms by which exercise can significantly increase your level of happiness and why it is an important inclusion within your Business Plan for Happiness.

The evidence, however, does not stop at the physical. Exercise is also associated with having a direct effect on mental well-being too. Exercise is shown to improve self-esteem and self-perception.[56] Exercise significantly improves general sense of well-being[13, 14, 15] and significantly reduces all causes of early death.[97]

Studies confirm that regular exercise also helps reduce mental ill-health such as anxiety and depression.[24, 68] In fact, the mental health benefits of regular exercise have been shown to be as effective at alleviating depression and anxiety as pharmaceutical interventions such as anti-depressants.[92, 9]

If you are inactive, living a sedentary lifestyle and doing little in the way of structured exercise, you are not fulfilling your true potential to be happy. It is that simple. If you evaluate your level of well-being as "good" whilst living a sedentary lifestyle then you have the potential to raise your well-being to "awesome!" with the introduction of exercise.

The best thing is…

… a small amount of exercise gives you a lot of benefits.

To improve health and happiness as a sedentary adult or maintain health as an already active adult, the research shows that you should aim to perform some form of exercise for 30 minutes at a moderate level of intensity every day or around 150 minutes each week.[118]

The term 'moderate' is subjective because what you rate as a moderately intense level of exercise will not be the same as your neighbours. As a very basic rule of thumb, 'moderate intensity' can be described as the level at which your body becomes warm and your heart rate is raised along with your breathing rate but you are still able to hold a conversation without having to take regular gasps mid-sentence. If this is too abstract for you, use the Exercise Exertion Scale (EES) at the end of this chapter to help you gauge your effort.

TAKE UP EXERCISE

In order to gain the maximum benefits, your exercise sessions should include bouts of aerobic exercise (non-weight based moderate and rhythmical exercises) that last for at least 10 minutes.

For those of you who have a good existing level of fitness you can halve your time exercising to a total of 75 minutes each week by increasing the intensity to a vigorous level (No. 8 or 'Hard' on the EES).

Over the first ten minutes of your exercise routine, gradually work your way up to level 5/6 on the EES to warm up* and maintain yourself at this level for the desired duration of your exercise session (recommended for 30 minutes).

*Warming up refers to getting your body moving and getting the blood flowing. Warming up is a vital part of your exercise programme because it causes an increase in oxygen delivery to the heart. Putting a jumper on and sitting by the fire with a Coco does not count as a 'Warm Up' I'm afraid.

NOTE: If you have any concerns about taking up any form of exercise or if you have an existing health condition, please consult your doctor.

How to get started?

The common mistake when starting up any lifestyle change is to attack it like a military assault with all guns blazing. For example, on New Years Eve most people have a list of changes and resolutions to be implemented on the morning of January 1st.

The key concept to get straight from the start is that exercise, and the entire Business Plan for Happiness, is truly a *lifestyle* change, which means something you are going to incorporate into your life for the rest of your life. Perhaps you have spent the past thirty or more years being sedentary and relatively inactive and so spending a few more weeks planning and preparing your new permanently more active future should be acceptable.

If it takes a year to ensure that you imbed your new, healthier and happier habits so that they become an enjoyable and natural routine for the rest of your longer and happier life, then surely it is worth one year of gradual implementation, yes? The investment to incorporate an exercise routine that suits you, fits easily around other commitments and you enjoy, is time extremely well spent.

The key to success; the four P's:

1. Plan
2. Prepare
3. Pace
4. Partake

Plan: The importance of goal setting

To attain lasting happiness and increased well-being, your activities should be linked with intrinsic motivation. Opposed to extrinsically motivated activities in which you take part because you are told to, intrinsic activities are those that you enjoy purely because you like doing it. You take part in intrinsic activity for your own sake and any other benefits you get from it is a bonus. The real motivation driving intrinsic activities is the simple fact that *you* choose to do them and *you* like doing them.

Research by Ken Sheldon[12] (et al.) highlights two key points when deciding what goals to choose to increase lasting well-being:

1. Focus should be on activities that increase growth and connection rather than money, beauty or pursuit of popularity.
2. Your goals should be important to you personally and not pursued on request or demand of other people.

Reflecting and adding to some of the points raised when discussing Flow, here are some specific points of consideration when starting your new exercise regime:

- What do you want to achieve? For the purpose of your Business Plan for Happiness, I would say that you simply want to introduce a level of exercise that helps increase your level of well-being and quality of life but remember, it is not about what I think, it is *always* about what *you* think.
- What exercise do you enjoy? If you do not know then it is time for to do some research and try something. Most gyms will happily give you a guest pass if you are considering joining. If you prefer to start a solo exercise programme then borrow/buy some exercise DVDs or local walking books or contact your local council to discover what exercise programmes run in your area. There are plenty of options and, like I said, physical activity and exercise are very closely linked. Some County Councils will run what are called Green Gyms. These are voluntary community based gardening or restoration projects. They are structured in such a manner to purposefully resemble exercise and therefore produce the very same type of physical and psychological benefits as exercise.

The bottom line is that you are planning to partake in this activity for many years to come. It may take several trials and errors before you find the routine that suits you best. There is no point continuing with one that you do not enjoy. Forget what other people say you should do, or what exercises some fitness guru says is best for you, if you do not enjoy it you are unlikely to continue doing it.

Your goal is to exercise regularly and enjoy your training sessions rather than see them as a chore that you feel you *should* do. Incorporate the Flow structure and find something that *you want* to do.

Prepare yourself:
- Invest in basic equipment: I do not mean the latest running or exercise gear costing hundreds of pounds but if you invest some time and money in preparation for your new exercise programme, you are much more likely to feel a sense of physical, emotional and financial investment in your decision.
- The one-month rule: Research suggests that it takes around twenty-one days of regular practise for a behaviour to become a habit which is why gyms offer one month free membership. Gym managers know that if they can keep you there for a month your gym attendance is likely to become habit and you will pay for full membership thereafter. Ultimately your activity becomes part of your identity and who you are. To some people this may seem like an alien concept but once you feel all the health and happiness benefits it will feel strange and unthinkable not to exercise.

Pace yourself:
- Both physically and psychologically, perhaps the most important element is to pace your exercise programme. If you pace yourself incorrectly, you will make things much harder for yourself and even do yourself more harm than good.

A very common mistake made with any lifestyle behaviour change is to approach it at full-steam from the start. On New Years Eve, the less wise person (and this has included me) will pledge to give up smoking, give up drinking alcohol, eat healthier, take up more exercise, spend more time with family, take up mediation, do more for charity and change career path, all on January 1st. No wonder most fail all resolutions by February!

Similarly with exercise, there is a common mistake to do too much too soon. It is a common trap to fall into and I call it the 'rushing & resting cycle'.

After years of relative inactivity you decide that you are going to get fit. The date and time is set for the following morning at 7am. You get up feeling motivated and determined. You leave the house with inappropriate and inadequate footwear, wearing old decorating trousers and a T-shirt won down the pub, but nevertheless, you are off running into the sunrise feeling like Rocky...until, a short while later you have to turn back, feeling sick and dizzy.

The next morning you are exhausted, your legs are sore and you cannot walk let alone run so you decide to have a rest day. Your legs remain tender for another day but by day three you are off once again running into the sunrise as far and as fast as you can. This time you push yourself even harder because your unanticipated rest day has put your fitness plan behind schedule.

Now you have to take a further three days to recover and the cycle begins once again but this time you have three days to catch up on. You think you should be feeling improvements by now but it still seems just as hard, so you push yourself even further. Eventually, and very quickly, you give up. You say that you tried it but felt tired and sore all the time and did not seem to improve.

The key to a successful, lifelong and progressive exercise regime is to avoid this rushing & resting cycle and to pace yourself from the outset. From your planning you will know where you want to be in say, one year's time, and then calculate how much you need to do in order to gradually pace yourself there in small stages.

We rarely listen to what our body is screaming loud and clear. We tend to do the opposite of what our body is telling us. For example, if you are tired, you may tend to push yourself to get through the tiredness rather than looking at your lack of pacing. You should not subscribe to the 'no pain, no gain' philosophy. Pain is your body telling you something is wrong. Listen to your body and if you are finding that your new exercise routine is leaving you exhausted, you need to adjust your pacing because you are falling into the rushing & resting trap. If you are experiencing pain whilst exercising, stop immediately and find out what the cause is or why you are experiencing pain. Pain in the shin can be due to inappropriate trainers. Muscular pain can be because your technique is incorrect or lack of post exercise stretching. Chest pain can be a warning sign too so, listen to what your body is telling you, do not be a pessimist and throw in the towel, be an optimist, seek advice from the appropriate health professional to discover the cause of your pain so you can implement a solution and carry on.

Perhaps the main challenge you will face with pacing is perseverance and discipline because if you plan, prepare and pace, you will feel as if you can always do more during your exercise session but notice how much quicker you progress.

Partake

- Following the previous steps within this chapter you will have thought about what you would like to realistically achieve for your new exercise programme. You have planned, prepared and you know how you will pace yourself properly to achieve your goal. You are aware that often you will need to enforce a level of self-discipline to avoid the rushing & resting cycle and stick to your planned pacing even if you feel as if you can do more. Everything is in place so now all you need to do is partake. Go do it!

Remember, regular exercise is one of the most fundamental things you can do to significantly improve your physical health and psychological happiness.

Once you have successfully planned your exercise routine, how do you keep it going?

ACTIVATE YOUR DISCIPLINE AND GRIT.

Cited in Positive Psychology,[69] Kate Hefferon and Ilona Boniwell suggest three key elements to the successful perseverance and longevity of behaviour change:

1) Self-discipline

2) Grit

3) Self-regulation

Self-discipline and perseverance is the key to success when implementing a new behaviour. Heffron and Boniwell[69] define self-discipline as: *The ability to choose successfully amongst conflicting impulses.*

When it is raining or windy outside and your daily twenty minute walk is pencilled in, your mind-created-self will convince you to stay indoors where it is warm, dry and sheltered. This will be in conflict with your true self, which is telling you to get out there and stop being a wimp or find an alternative exercise inside the house.

Research shows that if you can control yourself through application of self-discipline and grit, you are highly likely to be more successful in all aspects of life.[47]

Whereas self-discipline refers to your ability to choose between two conflicting impulses, self-regulation refers to the actual process you go through in order to make your choice between the two impulses.

To be successful at self-regulation you need to set yourself clear, well-defined standards to live by. You must be able to track your progress and you should monitor your energy levels to make sure you are not running your battery down. You need energy to keep your strength up and your willpower fully charged. So once again, listen to your body, rest when you feel the need to, get a good night sleep as often as you can and recharge your batteries.

When your mind-created-self implants doubt, remind yourself of all the benefits you will gain from your new positive behaviour. If your motivation is beginning to dwindle and you notice your self-discipline is becoming weaker, you must take action to regain your motivation. List all the benefits gained from your new exercise routine. Make a picture collage of how you will look and how you will feel in the future when you achieve your goals. Remember you must be doing this for yourself. Doing it for your family is commendable but to be successful and motivated for years to come, you must take part in activity that benefits yourself because this will benefit your family as a by-product.

If you are finding your activity is becoming dull and boring, change the routine, change the structure, adjust the challenge to make it stimulating for yourself once again. Remember the rules of creating Flow: To create a Flow state in any activity, you must be on the edge of your skill but still in control. If your activity has become boring, then you are not on the edge.

EXERCISE EXERTION SCALE

Using this scale, 1: being no exertion (as if seated) through to 10: being maximum exertion (only able to perform exercise for a few seconds). How would you personally rate your level of effort?

1. **No exertion (as if seated)**
2. **Very light exertion (as if pottering around the house)**
3. **Some exertion**
4. **light exertion (beginning to know that you are starting exercise)**
5. **Moderate exertion (feeling slightly more warm but still able to hold full conversation)**
6. **Somewhat hard (feeling warm and perhaps starting to perspire with breathing rate slightly elevated)**
7. **Noticing exertion: (Perspiring with breathing rate noticeably elevated)**
8. **Hard (Breathing rate is such that conversations are interrupted with gasps for breath)**
9. **Very hard (Conversation is virtually non-existent due to lack of breath)**
10. **Maximum exertion (Conversation impossible and exercise only possible for a few seconds before fatigue)**

END NOTE

- Do you want to live a more fulfilling life?
- Do you want to increase the happiness in your life?
- Do you want to go about your day with an increased level of lasting and deep felt contentment and joy inside you?
- Are you going to commit to this Business Plan for Happiness?

Now it is time to take action and implement the techniques in this book in a structured and concise way.

Use the technique summary table at the end of the this book and rate each of the techniques in terms of how much initial effort you feel each technique will cost you.

Once you have done this, calculate which techniques will bring you the highest income of happiness at this moment in time (**H.I.R - I.E.R**). These are the techniques you will begin to prepare, plan, pace and partake (The four P's) in to start your Business Plan for Happiness.

Choose just one technique at a time. Using the four P's it is time to incorporate the technique religiously until it becomes a habit in your life. Make sure your practise is well imbedded into your lifestyle before attempting to move onto the next technique on your list.

Make sure you know that you are making progress. Notice how you feel better and your sense of well-being increases. Read back through your positive journal and notice how your life is improving.

Notice how others respond better towards you and how you are able to achieve more.

Be an optimist because you are at the controls of your life so adjust, change and adapt your tactics to strive forward and flourish.

May your life be filled with much love, laughter and happiness

Anthony

For more tips, articles and practical material to help you increase your lasting happiness, visit www.wisemonkeytraining.co.uk

I.E.R:

Your initial effort rating (1 = minimal initial effort. 10 = maximum initial effort)

H.I.R:

Your happiness income rating (1 = minimal happiness income. 10 = maximum happines income)

H.I.R - I.E.R:

Deduct I.E.R from H.I.R to give you an overall happiness income for each technique. Use this to choose which techniques to start with.

I.E.R	H.I.R	H.I.R - I.E.R	Technique	Page
	8		Identify your baggage	19
	7		Watch your bad self	20
	8		Five steps to increase your Emotional Intelligence	22
	8		Gather yourself a gratitude stone	27
	7		Three strategies to maintain control	30
	9		Write a positive daily journal	37
	8		Visualize your best self	40
	7		The A.I.M approach	42
	8		Don't buy into negative Press. Subscribe to Positive News	49
	8		Change your moody self	57
	9		Challenge your negative self	58
	7		Use a mantra	59
	7		Create a manifestation board	61
	10		Daily meditation for at least 15 minutes	74
	9		Present moment mediation	
	9		Identifying your work values	87
	9		Identifying and using strengths rather than learned behaviours	93
	9		Random acts of kindness	110
	9		Your dedication to creating Flow	118
	9		Do what you enjoy doing rather than to get somewhere	120
	10		Be sociable	124
	10		Take up exercise	127
	8		Activate your discipline and grit	132

ABOUT THE AUTHOR

With over a decade of expertise and study in the field of psychology, applied positive psychology and neuro-linguistic programming, Anthony Peters has helped hundreds of people boost their existing level of happiness and eliminate the barriers that had previously held them back in life. Find out more about Anthony via:

www.wisemonkeytraining.co.uk

REFERENCES

1. Abramson, L.Y., Seligman, M.E.P and Teasdale, J.D. (1978) Learned helplessness in humans - critique and reformulation. *Journal of Abnormal Psychology*, 87(1):49-74

2. Adelmann, K. (1987) Occupational complicity, control and personal income - their relationship to well being in men and women. *Journal of Applied Psychology*, 72(4):529-37

3. AICR/WCRF (2007) *Food, Nutrition, Physical Activity and the Prevention of Cancer: a Global Perspective*, Washington, DC: American Institute for Cancer Research (AICR)/World Cancer Research Fund (WCRF).

4. Aknin, Lara B., Elizabeth W. Dunn, and Michael I. Norton. "Happiness Runs in a Circular Motion: Evidence for a Positive Feedback Loop between Prosocial Spending and Happiness." *Journal of Happiness Studies* 13 (2012): 347-355. Abstract

5. Aknin, Lara B., Michael I. Norton, and Elizabeth W. Dunn. "From Wealth to Well-Being? Money Matters, but Less than People Think." *Journal of Positive Psychology* 4 (2009): 523-27. Abstract

6. Allender S, Foster C, Scarborough P and Rayner M (2007) The burden of physical activity-related ill health in the UK, *Journal of Epidemiology and Community Health* 61: 344–8.

7. Argyle, M. (2001). The Psychology of Happiness. New York : Taylor & Francis

8. Babyak M et al. (2000) Exercise treatment for major depression: maintenance of therapeutic benefit at 10 months, *Psychosomatic Medicine* 62 (5): 633–8.

9. Babyak M et al. (2000) Exercise treatment for major depression:

maintenance of therapeutic benefit at 10 months, Psychosomatic Medicine 62 (5): 633–8.

10. Bandura, A. (1997) *Self-Efficacy: The Exercise of Control.* New York: Freeman Press

11. Barefoot Doctor (1998) *Handbook for the urban warrior: A spiritual survival guide.* Judy Piatkus (Publishers) Ltd

12. Ben-Shahar, T. (2008) *Can you learn to be happy? Happier.* McGraw-Hill

13. Biddle, S.J.H. And Mutrie, N. (2007) *Psychology of Physical Activity: Determinants, Wellbeing and Interventions* (2nd ed). London: Routledge.

14. Biddle, S.J.H., Fox, K.R., Boutcher, S.H. And Faulkner, G. (2000) *The way forward for physical activity and the promotion of psychological wellbeing.* In S.J.H. Biddle, K. Fox and S.H.

15. Boucher (eds) *Physical Activity and Psychological wellbeing* (pp. 154-68). London: Routledge

16. Boucher. S.H. (2000) *Cognitive Performance, fitness and aging.* In S.J.H. Biddle, K.R. Fox

17. Branigan,C. Fredrickson, B. L. Mancuso,R. A. & Tugade M. M.(2000) The undoing effect of positive emotions, *Motivation and Emotion* 24: 237-58

18. Brickman, P., Coates, D. And Janoff-Bulman, R. (1978) Lottery winners and accident victims - is happiness relative? *Journal of Personality and Social Psychology*, 36(8):917-27

19. Brunstein, J. (1993) Personal goals and subjective wellbeing: a longitudinal study. *Journal of Personality and Social Psychology*, 65:1061-70

20. Bryant, F.B., & Veroff, J. (2007) *Savouring: A new model of positive experience.* Mahwah, NJ: Lawrence Erlbaum Associates.

21. Burton, C.M. And Kind, L.A. (2004) The health benefits of writing about intensely positive experiences. *Journal of Research in Personality*, 38(2):150-63

22. Burton, C.M. And King, L.A. (2008) Effects of (very) brief writing

on health: the two-minute miracle. *British Journal of Health Psychology*, 13:9-14

23. Busseri, M.A., Choma, B.L. And Sadava, S.W. (2012) Subjective temporal trajectories for subjective well-being. *The Journal of Positive Psychology.* 7(1): 1-15

24. Camacho, T.C., Roberts, R.E., Lazarus, N.B., Kaplan, G.A. And Cohen, R.D. (1991) Physical activity and depression: evidence from the Almeda county study. *American Journal of Epidemiology*, 134(2):220-31

25. CAPP (2010). Technical manual and statistical properties for Realise2. Coventry, UK: CAPP

26. Charvet, S.R. (1997) *Words that change minds: Mastering the language of influence* (2nd ed). Kendall/Hunt Publishing Company

27. Chief Medical Officer (CMO) (2004) *At least five a week: Evidence on the impact of physical activity and its relationship to health*, London: Department of Health (DH)

28. Chiesa, A. (2009) Zen meditation: an integration of current evidence. *Journal of Alternative Complement Medicine.* 15(5): 585-92

29. Choi, Y., Karremans, H., and Barendregt, H. (2012) The happy face of mindfulness: Mindfulness meditation is associated with perceptions of happiness as rated by outside observers. *The Journal of Positive Psychology.* 7(1): 30-35

30. Chomsky, Noam (1956). "Three models for the description of language". IRE *Transactions on Information Theory* 2 (3): 113–124.

31. Chomsky, Noam (1965). *Aspects of the Theory of Syntax*. MIT Press

32. Christakis, N. And Fowler, J. (2009) *Connected: The Surprising Power of Our Social Networks and How They Shape Our Lives*: New York: Little Brown & Company.

33. Ciesa, A., & Serretti, A. (2009) Mindfulness-based stress reduction for stress management in health people: a review and meta-analysis. *Journal of Alternative Complement Medicine.* 15(5): 593-600

34. Clarke, A., and Clarke, A.D. (1976) Early experience: Myth and evidence. New York: Free Press; Rutter, M. (1980) *The long-*

term effect of early experience. Developmental Medicine and Child Neurology, 22, 800-815

35. Cohn, M. And Fredrickson, B. (2009) Broaden-and-build theory of positive emotions. In S. Lopez (ed.) The Encyclopaedia of Positive Psychology (pp. 105-10). Chichester: Blackwell Publishing Ltd.

36. Craig, C. (2007) Creating confidence: A handbook for professionals working with young people. Glasgow, UK: Cnetre for Confidence and Wellbeing.

37. Csikszentmihalyi, M. (1990) Flow: the Psychology of Optimal Experience. New York: Harper & Row.

38. Csikszentmihalyi, M. (1997) Finding Flow: The Psychology of Engagement with Everyday Life. New York: Basic Books.

39. Danner, D., Snowdon, D, and Friesen, W. (2001). Positive emotions in early life and longevity: Findings from the nun study. *Journal of Personality and Social Psychology*, 80, 804-813

40. Davidson, R.J., Kabat-Zinn, J., Schumacher, J. Et al. (2003) Alterations in brain and immune function produced by mindfulness meditation. *Psychosomatic Medicine*, 65(4):564-70

41. Diener, E. And Oishi, S. (2000) Money and happiness: Income and subjective wellbeing across nations. In E. Diener and E.M. Suh (eds.) *Subjective Wellbeing Across Cultures*. Cambridge, MA: MIT Press.

42. Diener, E., and Diener, C. (1996) Most people are happy. *Psychological Science*, 3, 181-185

43. Diener, E., Horowitiz, J. And Emmons, R.A. (1985) Happiness of the very wealthy. *Social Indicators Research*, 16:263-74

44. DOH (2000) *Let's Get Moving*. London: Department of Health

45. DOH (2000) *National Service Framework for Coronary Heart Disease*. London: Department of Health

46. DOH (2009) *Be active, be healthy: A plan for getting the nation moving*, London: Department of Health.

47. Duckworth, A.L. And Seligman, M.E.P. (2005) Self-discipline

outdoes IQ in predicting academic performance of adolescents. *Psychological Science*, 16(12):939-44

48. Dunn,E.W. Aknin, L.B. and Norton.M. (2008): "Spending Money on Others Promotes Happiness." *Science* 319 1687-1688.

49. Easterlin, B.L., and E. Carden (1998) Cognitive and emotional differences between short and long-term Vipassana meditation. Imagination, *Cognition & Personality* 18: 69-81

50. Eisenberg, D.M., Delbanco, T.L., Berkey, C.S. Kaptchuk, T.J., Kupelnick, B., Kuhl, J., et al. (1993) Cognitive behavioural techniques for hypertension: are they effective? *Annals of internal medicine.* 118:964-72

51. Emmons, R. A. & McCullough, M. E. (2003) Counting blessings versus burdens: An experimental investigation of gratitude and subjective well being in daily life, *Journal of Personality and Social Psychology* 84: 377-89

52. Eppley, K.R., Abrams, A.L., Shear, J. (1990) Differential effects of relaxation techniques on trait anxiety: a meta-analysis. *Journal of Clinical Psychology.* 45:957-74

53. Findler, M.J. and Cooper, H.M. (1983) Locus of control and academic achievement: a literature review. *Journal of Personality and Social Psychology.* 44: 419-27

54. Forehand, R. (1992) Parental divorce and adolescent maladjustment: Scientific inquiry vs. Public information. *Behaviour Research and Therapy*, 30, 319-328

55. Fowler, J. And Christakis, N. (2008) Dynamic spread of happiness in a larger social network: longitudinal analysis over 20 years in the Framingham heart study. *British Medical Journal*, 337:1-9.

56. Fox, K.R. (2000) Self-esteem, self-perceptions and exercise. *International Journal of Sport Psychology*, 31(2): 228-40

57. Fredrickson, B. (1998) What good are positive emotions? *Review of General Psychology*, 2, 300-319

58. Fredrickson, B. (2001) The role of positive emotions in positive psychology - the broaden-and-build theory of positive emotions. *American Psychologist*, 56(3): 218-26

59. Fredrickson, B. (2009) *Positivity: Groundbreaking Research Reveals how to Embrace the Hidden Strength of Positive Emotions, Overcome Negativity and Thrive*. New York: Crown.

60. Fredrickson, B., Cohn, M.A., Coffey, K.A, Pek, J. And Finkel, S.M. (2008) Open hearts build lives: positive emotions, induced through loving-kindness meditation, build consequential personal resources. *Journal of Personality and Social Psychology*, 95:1045-62

61. Froh, J.J., Kashdan, T.B., Ozimkowski, K.M. And Miller, N. (2009) Who benefits the most from a gratitude intervention in children and adolescents? Examining positive affect as a moderator. *Journal of Positive Psychology*. 4(5): 408-22

62. Galbraith, R. (1982) Sibling spacing and intellectual development: A closer look at the confluence models. *Developmental Psychology*, 18, 151-173

63. Gardner, H. (1983) *Frames of mind: The theory of multiple intelligence*. New York: Basic Books; Mayer, J., and Salovey, P. (2002)

64. Gardner, J. And Oswald, A. (2006) Money and mental wellbeing: a longitudinal study of medium-sized lottery wins. *Journal of Health Economics*, 26(1): 49-60

65. Goleman, D. (1995) *Emotional Intelligences*. New York: Bantam.

66. Govindji, R., & Linley, P.A. (2007) Strengths use, self-concordance and well-being: Implications for strength coaching and coaching psychologists. *International Coaching Psychology Review*, 2(2) 143-153

67. Harter, J.K., Schmidt, F.L., & Hayes, T.L. (2002) Business-unit-level relationship between employee satisfaction, employee engagement and business outcomes: A meta-analysis. *Journal of Applied Psychology*, 87, 268-279

68. Hassman, P., Koivula, N. And Uutela, A. (2000) Physical exercise and psychological wellbeing: a population study in Finland. *Preventive Medicine*, 30(1): 17-25.

69. Hefferon, K., & Boniwell, I. (2011) *Positive Psychology: Theory, research and application*. McGraw-Hill. Open University Press

70. Hefferon, K., Grealy, M. And Mutrie, N. (2009) Posttraumatic

growth and life threatening physical illness: a systematic review of the qualitative literature. *British Journal of Health Psychology.* 14(2): 343-78

71. Hefferon, K., Grealy, M. And Mutrie, N. (in press) Physical activity as a 'stellar' positive psychology intervention. In E.O. Acevedo (ed.) *Oxford handbook of Exercise Psychology.* Oxford: Oxford University Press.

72. Helliwell, J., Layard, R., and Sachs, J. (ed) (2012) *World Happiness Report.* The Earth Institute. Columbia University

73. Hiroto, D.S. and Seligman, M.E. (1975) Generality of Learned Helplessness in Man. *The Journal of Social Psychology.* 31(2): 311-327

74. Jose, P.E., Lim, B.T. And Bryant, F.B. (2012) Does savouring increase happiness? A daily diary study. *The Journal of Positive Psychology.* 7(3), 176-187

75. Kashdan, T.B., Biswas-Diener, R. And Kind, L.A. (2008) Reconsidering happiness: the cost of distinguishing between hedonics and eudaimonia. *Journal of Positive Psychology,* 3;219-33.

76. Keough, K.A., Zimbardo, G. And Boyd, J.N. (1999) Who's smoking, drinking and using drugs? Time perspective as a predictor of substance use. *Basic and Applied Social Psychology,* 21:149-64.

77. Keyes, C., Shmotkin, D. And Ryff, C.D. (2002) Optimizing wellbeing: the empirical encounter of two traditions. *Journal of Personality and Social Psychology.* 82(6): 1007-22

78. King, L.A. (2004) The Health Benefits of Writing About Intensely Positive experiences. *Journal of Research in Personality,* 38, 150-163

79. King, L.A., Hicks, J.A., Krull, J., and Del Gaiso, A.K. (2006). Positive Affect and the Experience of Meaning in Life. *Journal of Personality and Social Psychology,* 90, 179-196

80. Koydemir, S. & Schutz, A. (2012) Emotional intelligence predicts components of subjective well-being beyond personality: A two-country study using self-and informant reports. *The Journal of Positive Psychology.* 7(2): 107-118

81. Leonhardt, D. (2001) If richer isn't happier, what is? New York Times, May 19, B9-11

82. Levy, B.R., Slade, M., Kunkel, S. And Kasl, S. (2002) Longevity increased by positive self-perceptions of aging. Journal of Personality and Social Psychology, 83: 261-70.

83. Linley, A., Willars, J., and Biswas-Diener, R. (2010) The Strengths Book. CAPP Press, UK.

84. Linley, P. A., Nielsen, K. M., Wood, A. M., Gillett, R., & Biswas-Diener, R., (2010). Using signature strengths in pursuit of goals: Effects on goal progress, need satisfaction, and well-being, and implications for coaching psychologists. International Coaching Psychology Review, 5 (1), 8-17.

85. Loehr. J., and Schwartz, T. (2004) *The Power of Full Engagement: Managing Energy, Not Time, Is the Key to High Performance and Personal Time.* Free Press

86. Lyubomirsky, S. (2006) Happiness: Lessons from a new science. *British Journal of Sociology.* 57(3): 535-6

87. Lyubomirsky, S. (2008) *The How of Happiness: A Practical Guide to Getting the life you want.* London: Sphere.

88. Lyubomirsky, S., L. King, and E. Diener (2005) The benefits of frequent positive effect: Does happiness lead to success? *Psychological Bulletin* 131:803-55

89. Maddux, J. (2002) Self-efficacy: The power of believing you can, In C.R. Snyder and S.J. Lopez (eds) *Handbook of Positive Psychology* (pp. 277-87). New York: Oxford University Press.

90. Maddux, J. (2009a) Self-efficacy. In S. Lopez (ed) *The Encyclopaedia of Positive Psychology* (pp.874-80). Chichester: Blackwell Publishing Ltd

91. Minhas, G. (2010) *Developing realized and unrealized strengths: Implications for engagement, self-esteem, life satisfaction and well-being.* Assessment and Development Matters, in press.

92. Mutrie N (2000) The relationship between physical activity and clinically defined depression, in Biddle SJH, Fox KR and Boutcher

SH (eds) *Physical Activity and Psychological Well-being*, London: Routledge.

93. Myers, D. (2002). The funds, friends, and faith of happy people. *American Psychologist*, 55, 56-67

94. N.I.C.E (2006) *Four commonly used methods to increase physical activity: brief interventions in primary care, exercise referral schemes, pedometers and community-based exercise programmes for walking and cycling*, London: National Institute for Health and Clinical Excellence (NICE) public health guidance PH2.

95. Ostir, G., Markides, K., Black, S., and Goodwin, J. (2000) Emotional well-being predicts subsequent functional independence and survival. *Journal of the American Geriatrics Society*, 48, 473-478

96. Otake, K., Shimai, S., Tanaka-Matsumi, J., Otsui, K. And Fredrickson, B.L. (2006) Happy people become happier through kindness: a counting kindness intervention. *Journal of Happiness Studies*. 7:361-75

97. Paffenbarger, R., Hyde, R., Wing, A. And Hsieh, C. (1986) Physical activity, all-cause mortality, and longevity of college alumni. *New England Journal of Medicine*, 314:605-13

98. Park, C.L., Riley, K.E. And Snyder, L.B. (2012) Meaning making coping, making sense and post-traumatic growth following 9/11 terrorist attack. *The Journal of Positive Psychology*. 7(3): 198-207

99. Park, N., Peterson, C., & Seligman, M.E.P. (2004) Strengths of character and well-being. *Journal of Social and Clinical Psychology*, 23, 603-619

100. Petch, M.C. (1996) Triggering a heart attack. *British Medical Journal*. 312: 459-460

101. Proctor, C., Maltby, J. & Linley, P.A. (2009) Strengths used as a predictor of well-being and health-related quality of life. *Journal of Happiness Studies*, 10, 583-630

102. Rotter, J. (1966) Generalised expectancies for internal verses external control of reinforcements. *Psychological Monographs*, 80 (609)

103. Ryff, C.D. and Singer, B.H. (2006) Best news yet on the six factor model of wellbeing. *Social Science Research.* 35(4): 1103-119

104. Scheier, M. And Carver, C. (1987) Dispositional optimism and physical wellbeing: the influence of generalised outcome expectancies on health. *Journal of Personality and Social Psychology,* 55:169-210

105. Scheier, M. And Carver, c. (2009) Optimism. In S. Lopez (ed) *The Encyclopaedia of Positive Psychology* (pp.874-80). Chichester: Blackwell Publishing Ltd

106. Scheier, M. And Carver, C. S. (1992) Effects of optimism on psychological and physical wellbeing: theoretical overview and empirical update. *Cognitive Therapy and Research,* 16: 201-28

107. Schneider, R.H., Staggers, F., Alexander, C.N., Sheppard, W., Rainforth, M. Kondwani, K., et. Al (1995) A randomised controlled trail of stress reduction for hypertension in older African Amercians. *Hypertension.* 26:820-7

108. Seligman, M. (1998) *Learned Optimism: How to change your mind and your life.* Free press, New York

109. Seligman, M. (2002a) *Authentic Happiness: Using the New Positive Psychology to Realize your Potential for Lasting Fulfilment.* New York: Free Press.

110. Seligman, M. And Csikszentmihalyi (2000) Positive Psychology: An Introduction (Special issue) *American Psychologist,* 55, 5-14

111. Sheldon, K. And Lyubomirsky, S. (2006b) How to increase and sustain positive emotion: the effects of expressing gratitude and visualizing best possible selves. *Journal of Positive Psychology,* 1(2): 73-82

112. Sheldon, K. And Lyubomirsky, S. (2009) *Change your actions, not your circumstances: An experiential test of the Sustainable Happiness Model.* In A.K. Dutt and B. Radcliff (eds)

113. Sheldon, K. M. & Kasser, T. (2008). Psychological threat and goal striving. *Motivation and Emotion,* 32, 37-45

114. Shelle, R., C. (1997) *Words that Change Minds: Mastering the Language of Influence* (2nd Ed.). Kendall/Hunt Publishing Company

115. Staw, B., Sutton, R., and Pelled, L. (1994) Employee positive emotion and favourable outcomes at the workplace. *Organization Science*, 5, 51-71

116. Stefanyszyn, K. (2007). Norwich Union changes focus from competencies to strengths, *Strategic HR Review*, 7, 10-11.

117. Tammy C. Pannells & Amy F. Claxton (2008) Happiness, Creative Ideation, and Locus of Control. *Creativity Research Journal*. 20(1) 67-71

118. W.H.O (2010) Global Recommendations on Physical Activity for Health. World Health Organisation

119. Waterman, A.s., Schwartz, S. And Conti, R. (2008) The implications of two conceptions of happiness (hedonic enjoyment and eudaimonia) for the understanding of intrinsic motivation. *Journal of Happiness Studies*, 9:41-79.

120. Weuve J, Kang JH, Manson JE, Breteler MMB, Ware JH and Grodstein F (2004) Physical activity, including walking, and cognitive function in older women, *Journal of the American Medical Association* 292: 1545–61.

121. Wood, A.M., Linley, P.A. Maltby, J., & Hurling, R. (2010) *Use of positive psychology strengths leads to less stress and greater self-esteem, vitality and positive affect over time: A three-wave longitudinal study and validation of the Strengths Use Scale.* Manuscript submitted for publication.

122. Wrzesniewski, A., McCauley, C.R., Rozin, P., and Schwartz, B. (1997). JOBS, CAREERS AND CALLINGS: People's relations to their work. *Journal of Research in Personality*, 31, 21-33

123. Wrzesniewski, A., Rozin, P., and Bennett, G. (2001). Working, playing and eating: Making the most of most moments. In C.Keyes and J. Haidt (eds.), *Flourishing: The positive person and the good life.* Washington, D.C.: American Psychological Association

124. Xiong, G.L., & Doraiswamy, P.M. (2009) Does meditation enhance cognitive and brain plasticity? *Annals of the New York Academy of Sciences.* 1172:63-9

125. Yaffe K et al. (2001) A prospective study of physical activity and

cognitive decline in elderly women: Women who walk, *Archives of Internal Medicine* 161 (14): 1703–8.

126.   Zimbardo, G. And Boyd, J.N. (1999) Putting time in perspective: a valid, reliable individual -differences metric. *Journal of Personality and Social Psychology.* 77: 1271-88

127.   www.well-beingindex.com